ISRAEL:
Democracy's Neglected Ally
1943 to the Present

PIERRE VAN PAASSEN

Israel: Democracy's Neglected Ally
1943 to the Present

Based on "The Best-kept Secret of the War"
being Chapter Four of his *The Forgotten Ally*
with a new preface by Shmuel Katz

Edited by H. David Kirk and Ed Ephgrave

Pierre van Paassen ca. 1942

🔼 *Ben-Simon Publications*
Brentwood Bay, B.C. Canada and Port Angeles, WA U.S.A.

Ben-Simon Publications
USA: P.O. Box 2124, Port Angeles, WA 98362
CANADA: P.O. Box 318, Brentwood Bay, B.C. V8M 1R3

Printed on acid free and recycled paper; text set in Times Roman
Jacket design by Rita Edwards
Typography by Island ImageSetters, Sidney, B.C.   ·
Published simultaneously in Canada and USA
Printed in Canada by Rolex Plastics Mfg. Ltd.

Library of Congress Control Number: 2002111305

National Library of Canada Cataloguing in Publication
Van Paassen, Pierre 1895-1968
  Israel, democracy's neglected ally, 1942 to the present

  Reprint of: "The best kept secret of the war" in his Forgotten ally.
  Includes bibliographical references.
  ISBN 0-914539-11-6

  1. World War, 1939-1945--Jews. 2. World War, 1939-1945--
Palestine. 3. Great Britain--Foreign relations--Palestine.
4. Palestine--Foreign relations--Great Britain. I. Title. II. Title:
Forgotten ally.
DS126.3.V36 2002   940.53'5694   C2002-910682-6

TABLE OF CONTENTS

* Page numbers and colour appear as they were in the original edition.

Editors' Note

Why This Book?

The answer requires some personal words about your editors. Both of us are Canadians, but we come with different antecedents, training, and faiths. David is a Jew who as a boy got out of Nazi Germany; he became a sociologist. Ed is an Evangelical Christian raised in England; he is a printer. What brought us together was an interest in biblical history and Jewish national resurgence. When Yasser Arafat turned down Barak's offer and unleashed Intifada II, we wondered what we could do to help Israel and its people.

Happily we found a common focus in the work of the Dutch-Canadian journalist Pierre van Paassen who, during the Nazi era, had consistently worked for the Jewish people of Europe. The message of one of his books remains applicable today. *The Forgotten Ally* (1943) shows Britain, squeezed between victorious German armies, using Jewish volunteers who helped win the desert battles against Rommel. In that book Van Paassen notes that Britain's official war records mentioned neither the important services rendered by Palestine's Jewish community, nor the valor of its Jewish soldiers. Pierre van Paassen set the record straight, rescuing the truth about the Jewish sacrifices that helped the Allies win the war.

For this booklet we chose a chapter from the first edition of *The Forgotten Ally,* appropriately called "The Best-kept Secret of the War". What was no secret was the fact of Arab enmity and British indifference toward

the building of the Jewish national home. What Van
Paassen called a war secret was that the Jews of British
Palestine, having volunteered extraordinary services to
Britain, did not have that fact recognized in the official
war record. Younger Israelis may find it surprising that
for Jewish fortitude and valor there was little recognition in pre-state days. Today, the Jewish state is not only
a source of strength to its people, but the sacrifices it
requires of them have become a source of pride.

Naming The Book

Knowing how Israel was rejected as America's ally
during the Gulf war, how the U.N. conference at Durban denounced Israel as "racist", and more lately seeing Europe wallowing in anti-Israel rhetoric and economic boycotts, it seemed apt to call this book *Democracy's Rejected Ally.* But since over the decades of the
state's existence, and even before, the democracies' attitude toward participation by Jews varied, we have chosen the milder title *Israel, Democracy's Neglected Ally.*
Nevertheless, there has been a tendency to single out
Israel for quite unjust criticism. As shown in the cases
cited below, that pattern goes back a long way.

Two Examples

The events below characterize, as it were, the recur-
rence of unjustified criticism of Israel in the world community.

During September-November 1956 there occurred the
"Suez Crisis", when Nasser's Egypt closed the Suez
Canal to international traffic, threatening the commer-
cial lifelines of England, France, and Israel. When the
three powers attacked Egypt, the Soviets and the United

States demanded that they withdraw, an order with which they complied after having done considerable damage to Egyptian arms, personnel, and territory. But the major criticism was finally directed mainly at Israel. "The Soviet government newspaper *Izvestia*, branding Israeli leaders as 'an irresponsible handful of adventurers,' (said) that the Israeli invaders should be tried as war criminals."[1]

The second event occurred June 7, 1981, when "Israeli F-4 Phantom jets, armed with precision weapons known as 'smart bombs,' destroyed the Iraqi reactor as it was nearing completion and not yet stocked with nuclear fuel. The plant was being built with French and Italian aid, and a French technician was reported killed."[2] The raid strengthened Arab arguments for nuclear weapons to balance Israel's military power if not superiority. But anti-Israel rhetoric was not limited to Arab spokesmen. The *New York Times* (June 9, 1981) engaged in unreasonable criticism, calling Israel's surgical bombing of the Osirak reactor "inexcusable and shortsighted aggression." Though America has never officially acknowledged it, in the Gulf War Iraq was relatively easy prey to aerial penetration, thanks to Israel's preemptive ("inexcusable"? "shortsighted"?) strike a decade before.

The critical reception of Israel's conduct in the Suez and Iraq reactor crises has earmarks of a continuum. Again and again Israel is blamed for acts of self-defense that are taken for granted in the case of other states.

---

[1] *Chronicle of the 20th Century, Mount Kisco, N.Y.*, page 791
[2] *ibid*, page 1191

Pierre van Paassen's account of Palestine Jewry, peremptorily shorn of well-deserved war honors, appears like the old-fashioned, and currently renewed, anti-semitism of double standards.

Enter Pierre van Paassen

Now we turn to the history of an unusual Christian who, throughout the murderous Nazi era, showed himself a stalwart champion of the Jewish people. As author of the daring wartime critique of Great Britain, *The Forgotten Ally,* Pierre van Paassen is owed whatever acclaim may be due to *Israel, Democracy's Neglected Ally.*

PIERRE VAN PASSEN:
AN INTRODUCTION

You are about to become acquainted with the author of *The Forgotten Ally*, one chapter of which makes up most of this booklet. Raised in the Dutch Reformed Church, Pierre van Paassen early in his career as a journalist became interested in Jewish life and Zionism. That interest led him, before and during the Nazi era, to work almost incessantly for the hounded Jews of Europe. He died in 1968, but his consistent support for Jewish statehood gives us clues to where he would stand on matters of embattled Israel today.

Pieter (later Pierre), born in 1895 in Holland's ancient city of Gorcum, was the first of three sons of Adrian and Antonia van Paassen. In 1910, the parents decided to move the family to Canada, but Josinus, the youngest of the brothers, developed tuberculosis. Since Canada's immigration laws prohibited the entry of persons with a history of TB, the plans had to be changed. The parents would remain with the dying boy, while Pieter and his younger brother Tom would go ahead to Canada. So it happened in 1911. Pieter had just turned sixteen.

In Canada the boys first worked as farm hands, but after some months they made their way to Toronto. Pieter, wanting to become a minister like his grandfather and uncle, managed to enrol at Victoria College as a work-study student for the Methodist ministry. After two terms he was sent as assistant to the minister of three small churches in the town of Porcupine in the gold mining district of Timmins in Northern Ontario.

All seemed to go well until the nineteen-year-old hurriedly married a local girl pregnant with his child. The Methodist church fathers looked askance at a student's marriage not sanctioned by them and Pieter lost his hold on the desired clerical career[3]. Now the sole provider of a family of six (his parents, brother Tom, his wife Ethel and daughter Toni), Pieter found employment as clerk in a gold mine. Like many of his fellow workers, Pieter opposed the war, but in 1917, with conscription on the horizon, the multilingual youth enlisted, hoping to become an interpreter.

Instead, armies having their own logic, Pieter was sent to France as a member of a railroad track-laying battalion. A tunnel accident left him with a mangled left arm so that, when he was returned to Canada in January 1919, he reappeared with his arm in a sling and with the French first name "Pierre". In Toronto he found that his wife, probably at odds with the senior Van Paassens, had absconded and that, to care for 5-year-old Toni, they had sent for their 22-year-old niece, Coralie Sizoo, from Gorcum, Holland.

After some time at loose ends, Pierre was hired as a rookie journalist at the *Globe*. One day at Union Station he interviewed two priests, one French, the other German, who, after years as missionaries in Borneo, had emerged to find that their countries had been at war. The two friends poignantly asked: "should we have been enemies?"- a story that resonated with the rising anti-war sentiment and was picked up across the continent.

The priests' story gave Pierre his own by-line, which

---

[3] The marriage certificate gives his occupation as "formerly a minister."

led to an offer from the Atlanta *Constitution*, the American South's great liberal paper. Thus by 1923 Pierre, cousin Coralie, and daughter Toni, had made their home in Atlanta. It was there that Pierre, now a full-fledged newsman, became interested in Jewish issues. He had reported a talk by a visiting rabbi from New York who, having traveled to Palestine, had been deeply moved by Jewish pioneering, and had been converted to Zionism. The encounter with that rabbi, and subsequent contacts with Zionist leaders, led Pierre to becoming a protagonist of Jewish national resurgence.

At the *Constitution* Pierre launched a truly prophetic syndicated column "World's Window". In 1925 he was named foreign correspondent for the *New York Evening World,* stationed in Paris. Now he was indeed at the window of a world gearing up for war. With Mussolini's Italy modelling much of Europe's Fascist future and the Nazis on the move in Germany, Pierre's dispatches began to decipher the temper of the time.

In January 1931 the *New York Evening World* ceased publication, but Pierre remained in Paris, working first for the *Globe*, and then for its rival, the *Toronto Star.* Early in 1933, soon after the start of the Nazi era, he was in Berlin where, fluent in German, he talked politics with locals in and out of beer halls. Reporting what he saw and heard, he was arrested and accused of "atrocity propaganda". Here are some of those "false atrocity propaganda" headlines sent by Van Paassen to the *Toronto Star* in 1933:

Feb 25:   JEW IS BEATEN TO DEATH BY
          HITLERITES IN BERLIN
          Kill All Jews is Cry of Nazis"

Mar 14: JEWS FLEE FROM GERMANY, BADLY
BEATEN, THEY SAY
One Hundred and Fifty Reach Poland -
Some Head for France - Many Penniless

Mar 25: SCRIBE ACCUSED OF SPYING
BRUTALLY BEATEN BY NAZIS
Van Paassen Marched to Police Station -
Given Dose of German Mailed Fist -
"Don't Mention It"

Mar 31: NAZIS' REIGN OF BLOOD ECLIPSES
MASSACRES OF MEDIEVAL TIMES
Total of 115,000 Arrested, Held Without Trial
- Hundreds Slain - Others Tortured - Many
Driven Insane - Jewish Judge Beaten,
Mangled in Public

April 11: PUBLISHED ATROCITIES LESS OF
ONE TENTH OF TOTAL PERPETRATED
British and French Press Tell of Many More
Cases than Van Paassen - Denials Discounted
- Many German Liberals Fear for Lives if
Source of Information Bared

April 13: JEWS FLEEING BY HUNDREDS SEEK
ANY REFUGE OFFERED
Convinced Not a Single Semite Will Be
Safe in Germany - Censorship Savage.

The accusation of "atrocity propaganda" led to the banning of the *Toronto Star* and to Pierre's expulsion from Germany. In response the *Star* of April 24, 1933 showing Pierre and Adolf side by side, noted: PIERRE VAN PAASSEN IS NOT A JEW.

The article begins with:

> Because of Pierre van Paassen's exposure of the ruthlessness of Hitlerism, it has been said that he himself is a Jew and therefore is voicing Jewish partisanship. Mr. Van Passion was born in Holland of Dutch parentage.

and it ends with:

> when a moustache is put on, as on the accompanying photograph...there is a certain resemblance.

PIERRE VAN PAASSEN IS NOT A JEW

In the above layout, No. 1 is Mr. Van Paassen, while Hitler is shown in No. 2.

Adventures like these may have contributed to Pierre's beginnings as an author of books. In *Days of Our Years* (1939) he traced the forces that had conspired to destroy the peace of Europe, leading to World War II. In a chapter on Palestine he described how the Jewish community of Hebron was slaughtered during the Arab riots of 1929, instigated by the notorious Mufti of Jerusalem. Long a protegé of the British administration, that insidious agitator fled during the war to Berlin and, as an admirer of Hitler, raised an Arab battalion to fight with the Nazi armies.

Where Would Pierre Stand Today?

The Mufti's machinations bear a remarkable resemblance to Yasser Arafat's. That Pierre van Paassen was overtly critical of Britain's support of the Mufti suggests he would find it dismaying that the arch terrorist "Chairman Arafat" is hailed as a "Partner for Peace". And he would be dismayed by a great deal more.

Could we imagine the intrepid champion of the Jewish people under Nazi Germany's racist heel standing by silently when the UN conference at Durban labeled Israel "racist"? Instead, would he not have applauded the Evangelical Christian group, whose newspaper ads[4] so graphically showed how the Jewish state airlifted black Ethiopian Jews to safety in Israel?

Or could we imagine him being misled, like so many contemporary journalists, by the world-wide barrage of anti-Israel propaganda? His books *Days of Our Years* and *The Forgotten Ally* give more than hints of Pierre's consistent pro-Jewish partisanship and how he justified it.

In *The Forgotten Ally*'s chapter "The Best-kept

---

[4] See next page for a copy of the advertisements placed by the International Christian Embassy Jerusalem in answer to the Durban conference.

Secret of the War", Pierre accused Britain of suppressing the news of Jewish valor. The story of the young Jews from Palestine, volunteers for some of the most dangerous missions of the North African campaign, had been ignominiously omitted from the official war record.

That erasure resembles later instances of Israel-bashing; such as occurred after the attacks on Egypt during the Suez crisis and on Iraq's nuclear reactor.

In Conclusion

We wish to express our gratitude to Shmuel Katz, the eminent Israeli writer, for his generous gift of the new preface where he recalls Pierre van Paassen and his own part in the struggle for the creation of the Jewish state.

With the publication of *Israel, Democracy's Neglected Ally* we join in the wider effort to stem the growing tide of anti-Israel, anti-Jewish propaganda. To insure that this little book will be widely read, we are making information about it available on the internet[5].

It is our hope that Pierre's rear-view mirror images of Palestinian Jewry's bravery in war will help to bolster Israel's resolve to stand firm for its rights as a nation.

---

[5] See the Ben-Simon web page: www.simon-sez.com

"THE BEST-KEPT SECRET OF THE WAR"
Chapter Four of
THE FORGOTTEN ALLY
by Pierre van Paassen

A NEW PREFACE
by Shmuel Katz

It has been a moving experience to re-read Van
Paassen. He injected into the war episodes that he
recounts with all the verve of a dramatic novel. Writing,
as he was, while the war was still going on, there is the
shadow of a pattern. Indeed the pattern had first worked
itself out in World War One. It was when famous scien-
tist Aaron Aaronsohn and his sister Sarah headed the
Jewish spy ring NILI to help the British against the
Turks. The British Commander-in-Chief General
Allenby and his Staff, who all worked in close liaison
with Aaronsohn knew well the crucial contribution made
by NILI to the victory at Gaza in the fall of 1917, which
brought Allenby to Jerusalem. The appreciation they
expressed, and their high praise for the young men and
women of NILI, their intelligence reports and their
sacrifice - Sarah was tortured and committed suicide,
two of her colleagues were hanged - find no mention
whatsoever in the official British reports of the war.

Coming back to World War Two, it was evidently after
van Paassen had finished writing his book that official
confirmation was first published (in a speech by
Foreign Secretary Eden in Parliament) of the fate which

the "forgotten ally" was to suffer: condemned to death by the Nazis - without the British or Americans lifting a finger to save the Jews who could still be saved.

Then, the recognition of Jewish participation in the war was achieved only after a long struggle, towards the end of the war. The soldiers of the Jewish Brigade fought doughtily in the Italian campaign, but their better known achievement was elsewhere. Unbelievably, the survivors of the Holocaust, after their years of hell, were detained by the British in camps (Displaced Persons!) so as to prevent their coming to the Jewish National Home in Palestine. It was soldiers of the Brigade, evading British surveillance, who built up an organization (B'richa - 'Flight'), which smuggled them down to the coast and there onto boats of 'illegal' immigrants to Palestine - boats that did not always succeed in avoiding capture and some even forced to return to a Europe steeped in Jewish blood. The famous *Exodus* was one of these boats. Others, after capture, were detained in concentration camps in Cyprus until the British Mandate regime in Palestine came to an end.

The survivors who reached Palestine directly were able to join one of the underground movements actively fighting the repressive British regime with the aim of forcing it out of Palestine. Many of the underground soldiers had served as volunteers in the British army in North Africa and in Europe. They too were 'forgotten allies.' But they made up for it - by being remembered as among those (in the words of Rabbi Aba Hillel Silver) ".... without whom the Jewish State would not have come into being!"

ENDORSEMENTS 2002

Rabbi W. Gunther Plaut
Senior Scholar, Holy Blossom Temple, Toronto.

"I am much taken with 'Israel, Democracy's Neglected Ally.' Concise and clear, the little book is a 'must read.' Go and get it!"

Moshe Kohn
Veteran Jerusalem Post political, social and cultural commentator, Jerusalem.

This booklet might well be titled: "Pierre van Paassen: Israel's Neglected Friend." Kirk and Ephgrave deserve the Jewish people's gratitude for reviving the memory of one of Israel's greatest Christian friends. Van Paassen, one of the great journalists of the 20th century (he died in 1968 aged 73), was a passionate lover and active supporter of Zionism and Israel, because of his deep Christian faith and his equally passionate love of liberty and democracy. He expressed both of these loves in his numerous news dispatches from various parts of Europe and from Mandatory Palestine, in the latter instance relentlessly exposing British duplicity. I am especially grateful to the editors for reprinting in this booklet the chapter "The Best Kept Secret of the War" from Van Paassen's great 1943 book about the active massive participation of the Jews, especially the Jews of Mandatory Palestine, in World War II, The Forgotten Ally. After reading this booklet, you will want to go on to read The Forgotten Ally and his earlier books, especially Days of Our Years.

Professor Edward Alexander
University of Washington, Seattle.
Author of "THE JEWISH WARS: Reflections by One
of the Belligerents."

*"This excerpt from Van Paassen's 1943 account, given
with his characteristic passion and insight, not only in-
forms us about the large role that Palestinian Jews
played in enabling the British to keep Rommel from
conquering Egypt and severing Britain's lifeline; it also
reveals the perfidy and hypocrisy of the British in con-
cealing that role. And so it provides an eerie premoni-
tion of the moral debacle of the greedy and pusillani-
mous members of the European Union today when faced
with the Arab campaign to destroy Israel."*

Rael Jean Isaac
Editor of *Outpost*,
Americans For a Safe Israel, New York.

*"Canadian sociologist H. DavidKirk...has...importantly
issued, with Ed Ephgrave, an evangelical Christian,
Chapter 4 of Pierre van Paassen's The Forgotten Ally,
about the role Jews played during World War II in the
fight against Rommel's forces in North Africa, then on
the verge of overrunning Palestine and the rest of the
Middle East.
The paperback has a preface by Shmuel Katz and an
introduction by Kirk, who tells us their motivation in
reprinting this beautifully written, forgotten story of
Jewish heroism: 'It is our hope that Pierre's rear-view
mirror images of Palestinian Jewry's bravery in war
will help to bolster Israel's resolve to stand firm for its
rights as a nation.'"*

THE
FORGOTTEN
ALLY

By

PIERRE VAN PAASSEN

DIAL PRESS • NEW YORK • 1943

AUTHOR'S PREFACE

Since the war now raging is one of global dimensions, involving the future and destiny of all mankind, it may appear to some that the solution of the problems of so small a country as Palestine, will be but an incidental, if not a task of minor importance for the United Nations at some future peace conference. I have nevertheless made Palestine the central theme of this book.

I have done this because I do not believe that the defeat of the Axis will automatically solve the Jewish problem with which Palestine is intimately and inextricably bound up. For that question is in fact being settled now; on the one hand by the frightful and uninterrupted killing of Jews in Europe and on the other by the lack of interest in high places, both in Britain and in America, in providing the terrorized remnants of European Jewry with a means of escape or even with a ray of hope for survival.

In the welter of immense and vexing problems facing the United Nations in Europe, Asia, and Africa, especially in the world's traditional areas of colonialism, wherein Palestine is located, the present method of dealing with the Jews by reassuring them from time to time with saccharine but perfectly meaningless phrases and on the other hand by enforcing their exclusion from Palestine may well be, I am afraid, indicative of the manner and spirit in which other peoples' problems are to be dealt with by the secret diplomacy of an unregenerate imperialism.

THE FORGOTTEN ALLY

The fate of the Jews is being settled today by political events in the Near East and by decrees issued by Britain's Colonial Office. The new and better world that is to emerge from mankind's present agony is becoming visible in the Holy Land. It is not a happy or inspiring sight.

As one who is aware and who feels with a sense of personal involvement Christianity's guilt in the Jewish people's woes and the constant deepening of their anguish, I could no longer be silent. I made no emotional appeal. My language is not violent; the facts are. I simply stated the case of the Jews and their country for the consideration of all men of good will.

PIERRE VAN PAASSEN

CHAPTER 4

THE BEST-KEPT SECRET
OF THE WAR

IN the summer of 1942 the situation of the British army in Egypt was little short of desperate. It had lost more than half its man power and the better part of its mechanized equipment to Marshal Rommel, who was boasting openly that before six weeks were over he would-be sleeping peacefully in the royal suite of Shepheard's Hotel in Cairo. And why shouldn't the German commander have been confident that final victory lay within his grasp? Fortune's every augury pointed in his direction. The Egyptian plum seemed ripe for the picking. Rommel merely needed to stretch out his hand, so to speak, and the British Empire's life line was about to snap in twain. Hadn't he completely nullified Wavell's earlier conquests and hadn't he thrown Auchinleck out of Libya in one brilliantly executed stroke? One more such move, just one more such resounding blow by his perfectly co-ordinated Afrika Korps could scarcely have any other effect than sending the British reeling across the Canal or scurrying for shelter into the trackless wastelands of the Sudan . . . .

Rommel's scout planes were over the Nile Valley

and over Suez within twenty minutes after rising from the desert bases. Through his field glasses the Marshal could see the needle point of Pompey's Column in the heart of Alexandria as clearly as the minarets of the Mohammed Ali mosque, all of it less than seventy miles, less than a couple of good days' drive distant. He had ample cause to be hopeful of terminating the issue by one last determined push. The goal was in sight. He said one day that he was playing a game of cat and mouse with Montgomery and that he could make the kill whenever he chose to do so.

The Mediterranean sea lanes were dominated by land-based Axis bombers so that ships carrying reinforcements in men and material to Rommel's opponents were compelled to make the enormous detour around the Cape of Good Hope. Even so, less than half the new equipment from Britain and America succeeded in getting through the packs of submarines hunting off the South Atlantic coasts. On the other hand, Rommel's own, much shorter line of supply remained intact. By way of Italy, Sicily, Tunis, and Benghazi a steady stream of men, tanks, planes, oil, and munitions was pouring into his camp. What could the British do but fall back when the already victorious Italo-German machine was geared up once more and came rumbling forward?

Britain's plight seemed indeed irremediable. Her great cathedrals had crumbled under the mass assaults of the Luftwaffe. The one port after the other–Portsmouth, Southampton, Liverpool, Newcastle, Plymouth –had flared up in the night, turned into piles of smoking dust and ashes in the morning. Across the Channel, twenty-six miles distant, the German invasion barges lined the shores from Dieppe to Calais and from Ostend to Walcheren. The guns and the tanks that were to beat England into subjection were wheeling up along a hundred parallel roads leading to the Channel coast. Nazis stood massed in Holland, Denmark, France, Norway, and Belgium. America's supplies were still a mere trickle. What equipment could Britain spare for her armies in Egypt when her production had not made up for the losses sustained in the disaster of Dunkirk and when the Russian ally, now pressed back to the Volga line by Rundstedt's sledge-hammer blows, clamored in desperation for help? Singapore had fallen. The Japanese army was pouring into Siam and Burma. Corregidor had surrendered. The valiant Dutch navy had sunk beneath the waves. India was menaced, and Australia angrily insisted on the recall of her divisions and air force stationed in the Middle East.

While Rommel put the finishing touches to his pre-parations for the last battle, the bells of Berlin's churches were ringing in anticipation of the fall of Cairo and Jerusalem. The Duce ordered the Italian cities "smothered" under flags and bunting in joyous celebration over Britain's awful predicament. Young Blackshirts danced in the Piazza del Popolo. Not a word about the inhumanity and cruelty of aerial at-tacks came from Vatican City when it was a case of Protestant England being bombed to smithereens. Francisco Franco had his Phalangists demonstrate under the windows of the British ambassador in Madrid and shout their master's disdain for the rocking Empire of Britain with the cry: "Gibraltar! Gibraltar!" Over in

[177]

Paris and Vichy *ces messieurs* of the French General Staff and the new Nazi order, the Déats, Pétains, and Peyroutons, who had brought in the German armies to put an end to what Weygand once called "all this democratic nonsense," rubbed their hands in satisfied glee as the former comrade, now half blinded by sweat and blood, staggered on his feet. Their prophecies of England's fall were at last nearing fulfilment. The giant was groggy at last. The world's policeman was now obviously himself in a trap. They could hear his labored breathing. In Madrid, Vatican City, Tokyo, and Berlin they listened for the death rattle to begin.

In whatever direction they looked in that critical hour the British people saw little better than enmity, defiance, animosity, or sullen indifference to their fate. Isolationist moralists proclaimed from their platforms and in their press that now the transgressions of the fathers were being visited on the children, that England was getting her just deserts under the law of divine retribution. All the Empire's sins—in Ireland, in India, in South Africa—were held up to the public gaze. There were men in America who calmly envisaged the destruction of the British Empire as if that event would not have shaken the very ground from under their own feet.

It would have been a black day indeed for the human race, as Santayana once said, if scientific blackguards, conspirators, churls, and fanatics had managed to supplant Great Britain!

England stood alone. The world held its breath as a great empire seemed about to descend into the tomb. What is the mysterious power that sustained the

British people as they faced a seemingly inescapable disaster and the gates of doom with a stoicism and silent equanimity reminiscent of the *gravitas* of the Romans of the golden age? England stood against the world: flesh and blood against fire and steel. Yet not a whimper came from her lips. The English soldier, remarked a man who saw him, grows silent and faces death as if he shares a secret with his Maker. England was silent in the summer of 1942. It was her greatest hour!

But the crux of the desperate situation lay in the Near East. And there an ominous and sinister stillness prevailed at the British army's back. Young King Farouk of Egypt and his ministers had refused to lift one little finger in the defence of their invaded country. We know from diplomats who were in Cairo at the time that Nazi victories were commented upon with hopeful smiles and an exchange of meaningful glances in the palaces on the Nile. In Palestine the effendis (landed aristocrats) were telling the fellahin (peasants): "Now go and sell your land to the Jews and be quick about it, for in a month Hitler will be in Jerusalem, and you will not only have your land back but everything the Jews possess! Let the knives be sharpened! The great day is about to dawn! The Jews' protector is beaten!"

Twenty-four hours of the day the radio stations of Bari, Palermo, and Berlin were screaming the promises of Mussolini–the "Sword of Islam"–in the Arabic language: "Loot immeasurable, death to the English and Jews!" The two honored guests of Adolf Hitler–the ex-Mufti of Jerusalem, Haj Amin Effendi El Husseini, and the ex-Premier of Iraq, Rashid Ali-el-Gailani Bey, announced their speedy return and a settlement of old scores. In the mosques of Baghdad, Cairo, Amman, Jerusalem, Damascus, and Mosul, a careful investigation revealed, ulemas and muftis time and again working up the believers to a frenzy of excitement by pointing to the nearness of the hour of quittance in blood with all the *roumis* and infidels.

Let us have done with the preposterous myth of the Arabs eagerly waiting for an opportunity to rush to Britain's aid! The truth is that the so-called Arab world —that is to say, the princes, potentates, imams, mullahs, and emirs—were yearning to stab Britain in the back. King Ibn Sa'ud, who was suddenly to declare himself an ally of Britain and America, had not a word to say and could not spare a single trooper, camel, or donkey when Rommel stood at Alamein. The Imam of Yemen had to be watched constantly. Both princes received subsidies from the British government to keep the peace. In Iraq, whose attempt to oust the British garrison and hand over the Mosul oil fields to Germany had just been defeated, the instructors and students at the War College in Baghdad, as one British Intelligence officer relates, were still regretfully lamenting, a year after the event, their failure to establish contact with Nazi paratroops at the time of the revolt.

Had one German division set foot on the Syrian or Palestinian shores, the British command in Egypt would have had a conflagration at its back running from the Persian border to the Hadhramaut and Aden. As it was, almost as many British troops were required to patrol the doubtful Arab areas and cities, especially in Egypt, than there were actually facing Rommel's Afrika Korps in the Libyan desert . . . .

Not only in the Near East were the prospects utterly gloomy; the skies were darkening everywhere. Just as Rommel was stealing up and crouching for the last leap at Suez to cut the British Empire's jugular vein, the Red army received the full impact of Hitler's concentrated attack in the Donetz Basin. Timoshenko was forced to abandon Russia's most powerful industrial area, the richest coal mines, and the strategic railroads of the Caucasian transportation system. Sevastopol fell. Novorossisk followed and the entire Kuban district. The Nazis were pouring from the Crimea into Caucasia. They were marching around the shores of the Black Sea. In a few weeks' time they stood in the passes of the Caucasus Mountains within sight of Russia's refineries and oil fields. They were on the point of seizing those raw materials which would have enabled them to go on fighting indefinitely.

Men are apt to forget, now that the design has been gloriously frustrated by General Montgomery, that the pretentious objective of the Axis in the Near East was to cut the British Empire in twain by bringing about a juncture of German-Italian naval power with Japan's via the Mediterranean, the Suez Canal, the Red Sea, and the Indian Ocean. Every German strategist of importance attributed Germany's defeat in the war of 1914-1918 to the fact that British naval power had succeeded in throwing an impassible cordon of steel around the Reich, thus depriving it of the raw materials with which modern wars are fought. If the Germans in the First World War had been able to reach and draw

upon the stocks of Asia and Africa, the analysts of the
defeat were convinced, an entirely different story would
have been told in the Hall of Mirrors at Versailles in
1920.

The supreme and costly error in the calculations of
the Kaiser's grand strategists, it was discovered, lay in
the neglect of the German High Command to support
the Turks adequately in their drive on Suez in 1915
and in not pursuing the Near Eastern objective by a
campaign of more determination and magnitude. Egypt
and Palestine were the British Empire's most vulnerable
spot, the solar plexus of its global defence system.
There, in the neighborhood of the Canal which linked
the British motherland with the reservoirs of wealth
and man power in the East and the Antipodes, where
"the thin red line" was thinnest and most dangerously
exposed, the blow could have been struck that would
have doubled the Empire back on itself and made the
infliction of a mortal wound possible.

The fundamental error was, Generals Ludendorff
and Buat admit in their memoirs, that too many divisions were diverted to the Russian front instead of
being sent to the support of Turkey in Asia Minor
and in the Arabian Peninsula. The Turks, after a
brief offensive show, were neglected and allowed to
shift for themselves. They, too, turned their attention
towards Russia, confining themselves to defensive operations in the Near East, whereas they should have done
the opposite: attack in Egypt and be content with defence in the Caucasus. Russia, after Hindenburg's
crushing victories at Tannenberg, the Masurian Lakes,
and in the Carpathians, was disintegrating rapidly and

could have been held in check with a relatively small effort. On the Eastern Front huge German forces lay immobilized for years while victory's prize lay in another direction. German strategy mistook that direction for a mere diversion and treated the war in the Near East as a side show, whereas Germany's major efforts should have been concentrated on Arabia and Egypt, on driving the British from the eastern entrance to the Mediterranean.

But if that mistake had been made in 1914-1918, it was not to be repeated in 1939. If the German armies failed to reach the wealth of Asia and Africa once, they were to do better next time. New weapons, new tactics, a new spirit, a bold strategy of global dimensions would, so it was figured, overcome the obstacles that had formerly barred the Reich from its place in the sun. Air power was the new weapon. The new Germany of Hitler would wing itself over the walls of steel that British naval power might throw up again around the Reich or around a German-controlled Continent.

In the new conception of strategy, elaborated under the Weimar Republic which left the old General Staff undisturbed, and adopted as the official fundamental doctrine of war upon Adolf Hitler's accession to power, the conquest of the European *Herzland* was a preliminary move on the road to world power. This Britain could not prevent and might even consent to if Germany's secret objective were presented as the colonization of Bolshevik Russia. With the rapid collapse of France, it turned out a relatively easy undertaking. Europe fell under the German heel. But the real objectives in the new war the Germans unleashed lay beyond. Africa and Asia were the essence of the Greater Germany's *Lebensraum*. These two continents, which were renamed Eurafrica and Eurasia in the new geopolitical strategy–that is, mere economic adjuncts of the German-controlled European "heartland"–were the principal goals Germany aimed at in her new bid for world power.

By occupying or gaining control of the principal bases and sea lanes of Africa it was clear that the South American continent, too, would inevitably fall within the orbit or at least be drawn within the sphere of influence of the Third Reich. Without gaining control of the Mediterranean, which was, in the conception of Dr. Haushofer, the theoretician of the new geopolitical school, not a barrier of water separating Europe from Africa but the link binding these two continents together, a mere inland lake of Eurafrica, and without control of the South Atlantic sea lanes and the resources of Africa and western Asia, the conquest of Europe would remain a sterile victory, an incompleted effort in that the Reich could never hope to fulfil its ambition of becoming the all-dominating industrial and the one unchallengeable military power in the universe.

Only a few men in the democratic countries were aware of how near Germany came to translating that fabulous dream into reality. President Roosevelt was one who early grasped the stupendous magnitude and significance of the plot. Yet the very fantastic nature of the project, the gigantic scope of the German imagination, would have turned a description or analysis of it on his part into a cause for raillery and opposition to his preparations for defense. The vast German scheme, even when it was being worked out with startling precision before their eyes, escaped the comprehension of his parochial-minded opponents, who sought refuge in ridicule and irreverent demagogic wisecracks. The President had to content himself with the oft-reiterated warning that America was in grave danger, without specifying the exact nature and size of that danger.

Unprepared and almost defenseless, America was in a fair way of being taken in a gigantic, hemispheric pincer movement, with the European-African coast on the one side and the coast of Asia on the other representing the two arms of the nutcracker. A bridge of air power that could be thrown across the Atlantic between Dakar in Vichy's hands and the bulge of Brazil further emphasized the perilous position of America. By stirring up trouble in South America and massing air power there, the Germans planned to throw America back on a defense of the continental United States only, avoiding a frontal attack on the defenses of the Panama Canal by outflanking them, as they had outflanked the Maginot Line, and to launch their invasion of America by way of the Gulf of Mexico and the Mississippi Valley. Once or twice the staggering military plot that Germany hatched against the United States was revealed by certain periodicals and analysts, only to be dismissed by the public as too fanciful and preposterous and too farfetched. Isolationists ridiculed the idea that America was in any danger at all.

How near Germany's geopoliticians and military strategists came to fulfilling that bewildering dream of theirs men will probably not realize until the secret history of the war is written. For two years the German armies moved irresistibly and with inexorable determination towards their goal. The Czechoslovakian fortress jutting into the Reich's most vulnerable flank was removed by an adroit political maneuver. Tory Britain was successfully hoodwinked in believing that with the removal of that bulwark Germany's road to the Russian East was cleared. Poland was eliminated in one stroke. France fell. The gallant armies of Yugoslavia and Hellas were overwhelmed. The brown legions surged victoriously through the passes of the Thermopylae and filled the peaceful Peloponnesus with the metallic clatter of their assault cars. In a month they were in Crete, halfway across the inland lake of the Mediterranean.

In the slim finger tips that Hellas dips into the sea in Laconia, nature herself seemed to point the way to the gray hosts that poured through the Balkans for the shores of the old world sea. With the arrival of the German army in Marseille shortly before, the two main roads to Africa had been cleared. The great objective was in sight. Within a month the Germans had occupied the Cyclades and thus extended a bridge to the isle of Rhodes where Mussolini had been teaching landing tactics to his Army of Asia. From Mount Carmel in the Holy Land, men were daily scanning the skies expecting to see landing parties approach from Cyprus across the bay. Messerschmitts and Junkers roared over Nicosia bound for Beyrouth and Damascus, where German technicians were helping the Vichy French to lay out new airdromes. The ground for the invasion of the Syrian coast was prepared. Discerning spirits everywhere in the world recognized that one of the decisive hours in history was about to strike.

In the border areas of Europe and Asia, as much as on the borders of Asia and Africa, it was for the German High Command, merely a question of one more determined push in June, 1942, of delivering one more crippling blow: the *coup de grâce*. Like the arms of a monstrous octopus–Rommel on one side, Von Rundstedt on the other–the German armies were enveloping the whole Near and Middle East in a seemingly irresistible nutcracker movement . . . .

At that moment, it may now be revealed, the British High Command thought the game was up. Winston Churchill personally telegraphed the military authorities in the Near East to construct a set of bridges across the Tigris and Euphrates Rivers in Iraq. His order had precedence over all other pending tactical plans or defense projects. London feared a simultaneous German break-through on the Nile at Alexandria, on the Volga at Stalingrad, and in the Caucasian Mountains near Baku and Tifflis. If that had happened, it must be obvious that the British armies in the Near East would have been cut off. In the event of a break-through and of the two German armies converging towards each other, through Syria from the north and through Sinai from the south, there was no other solution but to retreat, if the British armies were not to be caught between two fires and annihilated. It was therefore planned, if the break-through occurred, to abandon the Suez Canal, Sinai, Palestine, Lebanon, Trans-Jordan, Syria, and Iraq and to attempt a retreat in the general direction of Persia. To facilitate the retreat and save as much matériel as possible, bridges were to be thrown over the two great Mesopotamian rivers.

But where could they get the steel and the material and the technicians and the crews of workers to build those bridges? The British army in Egypt could not spare a single engineer. Material was not known to be any nearer than Leeds or Birmingham . . . . After a few days' deliberation, British military commanders in Egypt and Syria were on the point of notifying London that the plan could not be carried out and that another scheme for the retreat must be provided at once.

It was at this moment that a Jew from Czechoslovakia, a businessman who lives in Palestine, happened to come into the office of the British military commander in Jerusalem. The Jew had come to get the commander's signature to an order of sheet metal which his small plant manufactures. As he sat in the antechamber of the general-headquarters building in the old Russian Compound, he saw several officers come out of the conference room. When he was summoned to come in himself, he found the harassed-faced commander bent over a map of Iraq and sighing disconsolately: "It can't be done! My God, I don't see how it can be done!"

A reliable and highly placed informant in the Middle East told me that the Jew hesitatingly inquired what the trouble was, whereupon a dialogue along the following lines developed between the two men. The commander explained first the predicament he was in: the immediate vital need of bridges in Mesopotamia, the lack of experts and material . . . . "I am afraid we are caught," he said, biting his fingernails.

[188]

"No," said the Jew, "we are not . . . ."

"If those bridges aren't built we are definitely caught," repeated the commander, as he looked his visitor straight in the eyes, with defiance almost. "The British armies are in a trap. There is no other word for it."

"If you let me, I will build those bridges for you," said the Jew.

The Englishman looked up. His jaw dropped. "You?" he said. "Do you know what is involved? Do you realize that this is an engineering feat of the first magnitude, the Euphrates, mud flats, miles wide . . . . Did you ever build a bridge before?"

"Yes," said the Jew, "I built two bridges, two of the largest in Europe, one over the Danube and one over the Moldau in Czechoslovakia . . . . I also built the subway in Berlin . . . ."

"Great God, man!" exclaimed the Englishman, jumping from his chair and seizing the Jew by the arm, "Do you know what you are saying?" And again he explained the fearful plight of the British armies.

"Yes," said the Jew, "we are all in a terrible fix, if there is a break-through . . . . Our old people, about a third of Palestine's Jewish population, carry poison in their pockets . . . . ready to die. Our young people will fight to the last, to the bitter end, of course. But we all know that the civilians cannot be evacuated . . . . Still, the army must be saved . . . . If you give the word, I will build the bridges."

"Where will you get the men?"

"Leave it to me!"

"Where will you get the material?"

"Leave it to me!" came back the Jew again. "Just let me go to Iraq and have one good look, and I will tell you in a few days how soon the job can be done . . . ."

It was left to him and the bridges were built.

A month before British forces invaded Syria, where the Vichy regime was smoothing the way for a German invasion, twelve Jewish boys answered the secret call of the British military authorities in Jerusalem to undertake the hazardous job of blowing up the oil installations in the port of Tripoli in Syria, the terminus of the French branch of the Mosul pipe line. British soldiers could not be sent, as France and Britain were not at war. Moreover, the raiders had to be men who understood both French and Arabic, as circumstances might force them to spend a considerable time in Syria before they would have an opportunity of approaching the refineries, which were, of course, under heavy guard.

The Jewish boys who volunteered were told that not only must they not expect a reward or recognition in the event of a successful conclusion of the raid, but that Britain would have to repudiate and even denounce them as spies and saboteurs if they were caught. If they should be captured and put to torture, they were told they were not to divulge who had sent them on their mission of destruction. They were commanded to take the secret with them into death . . . .

Under command of a British officer, the twelve volunteers worked out their own plan of attack and one night dashed off from Haifa in a speedboat crammed with high explosives. They came undetected, through the crowded harbor of Tripoli, got ashore and found their way to the oil installations, overpowered some French guards, and started their work of demolition. The alarm was given at once, and they were surrounded while still busy setting fires and tossing their bombs around. There was no chance of getting back to their boat. It is not known whether they were formally executed or cut down on the spot. After the British occupation of Syria remnants of their bodies were found in a shallow grave near the shore and identified by Hebrew lettering on the clothing. Then only were their parents informed of their death and sacrifice by the Palestine administration. And their relatives were informed at the same time not to expect any premiums or pension money, as the boys had not been regular British soldiers.

When the First Brigade of the Free French, mainly composed of foreign Legionnaires, after marching north through the Sahara from Fort Lamy on Lake Chad, was trapped by Rommel at Bir Hacheim,* in Libya, in June, 1942, and there, clamping itself to the bare rocky soil, performed the miracle of another Verdun by holding the line for Montgomery for a whole month during the most critical stage of the battle of Libya, repelling daily mass assaults by tanks and undergoing almost hourly bombardment by huge flocks of Stukas, a company of Jewish engineers belonging to the King's West African Rifles went through the same experience at Mechili, fifty miles to the east. The Jewish military

*L'Epopée de Bir Hakim, by Jean-Pierre Besnard, Les Oeuvres Nouvelles, Editions de la Maison Française, Inc. New York.

epic is related in the communiqués of General Koenig of the Free French. They were spotted by German scout planes as they were laying down a mine field which was to be a bar to possible attempts by Rommel to turn the flank of the Eighth Army as it stood with its back to Alamein. The Nazi observers caught sight of the Jewish engineers working in the open desert, swooped down to strafe them, and then flew off. That was on June 1. The next two days the whole plain around Mechili was blotted out in a whirling, yellow sandstorm which made the working party invisible from on high. The Jews could hear the Messerschmitts and Junkers roaring above the clouds of dust and apparently looking for them. Visibility on the ground was down to absolute zero.

Mechili is a stretch of flint-strewn sand with lava outcroppings, bordered on the east by the first undulating sand dunes of the Sahara. It is not an oasis, as some dispatches have made it out to be. Here and there you find a clump of burnt shrubbery, the color of ocher, but no trees, no shade, nothing but scorched desolation—sand and rocks. There is a well there, however, at which I stopped for a night in 1934 on my way back from Fort Lamy whither I had accompanied the scientific expedition of Professor Charles Perrault that was investigating the causes of the unexplained phenomenon of the sinking of the level of Lake Chad.*

The Jewish company's task in that area was to lay down a mine field in the shape of a quadrangle on a surface four miles by three. On the borders of the field

---

*Days of Our Years, Garden City Press, New York, page 252 et seq.

the mines were buried two yards apart; farther inside the field they were more widely spaced. Those mines are the size of a soup plate and consist of a metal box filled with an explosive. They are placed in a hole and then covered up. In a few days' time the sand levels the earth and no visible trace is left of the deadly machine. Such mines are designed to halt trucks weighing over five hundred pounds, tanks, and artillery. They do not explode when a man walks over them.

The engineers had scarcely begun their work, tracing the outline of the mine field by driving down stakes and connecting them with barbed wire when the Germans spotted them. As soon as the sandstorm subsided sixty heavy bombers paid them a visit and blew up half of their trucks. When the Stukas returned the following morning and twice more in the course of the afternoon of June 4, the officer in charge of the mine-laying operations, Major Felix Liebman, a citizen of Tel Aviv, heliographed the nearest British post for some antiaircraft guns. The answer came back that ten antiaircraft guns would be sent immediately, plus some antitank guns, as the Jews must be prepared to face a land assault any moment. British scout planes had observed a column of Nazi tanks moving in the direction of Mechili. With that message came word from the Commander in Chief himself, General Sir Bernard Montgomery, to finish laying the mines and to hold the field at all costs. The very fact that the Germans were paying so much attention to Mechili showed the importance they attached to the place. Reinforcements, too, were promised.

But these never arrived. In three days' time Mechili

was surrounded on three sides by a ring of enemy tanks, both German and Italian, and the engineering garrison was cut off from all contact with the outside world. Before attacking, the German brigadier in charge of operations sent a tank with a white flag and the message to hoist the signal of surrender. That happened on the morning of June 10. Major Liebman said to the German officer who brought the message: "We have no white flag! All we have is the banner. This we are going to fly. It's the blue flag of Zion! . . . ."

"Sie sind Jude" (You are a Jew), said the German in surprise, clicked his heels, saluted, and walked off.

Six hours later the tanks came rumbling towards the position, sixty in one column and twenty-five each in two others. A flock of Stukas which appeared simultaneously was forced to drop its bombs prematurely when it was attacked by British Kittyhawks. But the tanks rumbled on. The Jews held their fire until the first metal masters reached the barbed wire stakes. Then they let go. Two tanks blew up when they struck mines; nineteen were hit by antitank fire. One Jewish sergeant alone accounted for seven of them.

Meeting with so much unexpected resistance, the main tank column, which belonged to the Italian Ariete Division, halted, signaled to the others, and started to withdraw. This was the moment for which Major Liebman had prepared. Sixty of his men who had been hidden in dugouts near the extremities of the mine field rushed out when the Italians turned tail and bombarded the retreating tanks in their vulnerable rear with hand grenades, bottles filled with gasoline, and tommy guns. Some of the Jews jumped on the

back of the tanks, firing their revolvers into the lookout slits and gun holes. In this way five more enemy
machines were accounted for. As the last Italian cater-
pillars moved off British fliers swooped low over the
mine field and waved their hands at the Jews.

The following day the Germans subjected Mechili
to a merciless aerial bombardment. They repeated the
assault twice a day. They had apparently decided to
reduce the position by air attack, wipe out the little
garrison, and clear a path for their tanks around the
leftmost extremities of Montgomery's flank. For seven
days the bombs rained down, turning the mine field
into a wailing hell of steel in which it did not seem
possible for human nerves or human life itself to en-
dure. One squadron of Stukas had not passed over and
dumped its ghastly load before the next one winged
into sight. They dive-bombed the trucks, the dugouts,
the guncrew. They churned and plowed up the mine
field, filled it with craters two stories deep until Mechili
was an inferno of boiling red-hot, iron missiles in an
inferno of blistering desert heat. Still the Jews held out.

On June 20 the tanks returned en masse. Upon their
approach the weary, hungry defenders clambered out of
their foxholes and manned the guns. Again they re-
pelled the assault of the Ariete Division while an
aerial battle went on above their heads and British
fighters drove off the Stukas come to administer the
coup de grâce to the garrison. But at the end of that
day, although forty-one smoking tanks testified to the
deadly accuracy of the Jewish gunners, only ninety
men were left out of Major Liebman's original five
hundred.

Ten more days passed. Each day the Italians renewed the attack, raking the mine field with a murderous fire, getting nearer and nearer to the central position with each onslaught. Then the water well was hit and stove in by a well-placed Stuka bomb, and the agony commenced. From that day on the men were reduced to a daily pint of water from the tin cans dropped by the R.A F.

Major Liebman had banded his men closely together around the deep, central dugout. Here they were going to make their last stand. Outside lay the bodies of their comrades which the Stukas would not leave buried but plowed up and sent up in the air in a ghastly, maddening dance of rotting flesh and bones. Two men went out of their minds on June 25, two more the next day. Three men rushed off shrieking into the desert. The bombardment continued. With the summer heat mounting every day and the scorching wind blowing up clouds of dust, the men's thirst grew unbearable. Some drank gasoline and perished. Other drank their own urine and went mad with the pangs of greater thirst afterwards. Nobody spoke a word those last days. Rifles grew burning hot in the men's hands. The dive bombers sent up geysers of sand around them.

Forty-five men were left on July 1, a handful of unrecognizable scarecrows, scarcely human in appearance, unkempt, haggard, covered with grime, emaciated, some stark naked, having had the clothes blown off by the concussion of five-hundred-pound bombs exploding near by.

On July 2, they faced their last assault at six in the morning, lost two more men, and put the Italians to flight once more. At ten o'clock, a lookout man, who could scarcely speak, his tongue cleaving to the roof of his parched mouth, warned Major Liebman that a column of trucks was approaching, led by an automobile bearing the tricolor of France. The commander, although wounded in the head and in the groin, staggered to his feet and waved the answering signal.

The French troopers approached. They were the remnant of the Free French from Bir Hacheim who had received orders to withdraw the night before. The Jews stumbled into the open, looking like so many tortured ghosts. General Koenig of the Free French walked up to Major Liebman and embraced him. *"Vous avez tenu bon, jusqu'au bout,* you held out till the end," he said. Then tears choked the Frenchman's voice.

The Jews were given water, and the Major informed them that they were to accompany the French column. The siege was over. French soldiers were loading the remaining equipment on trucks. A flock of Spitfires sailed by, the pilots waving their helmets.

One Jewish soldier took down the blue and white flag of Zion, rolled it up, and was about to place it in its holder when General Koenig saw him and asked him a question.

"We are not permitted to fly that flag," explained Major Liebman. "It's against regulations . . . ."

"Pardon," said General Koenig, "I am in command here. *Je m'en fous pas mal des régulations,* I don't care a damn about regulations . . . . That flag goes on my car in front, next to the tricolor. That's where it belongs. *Nous sommes victorieux, tous les deux,* we have

[197]

both come through victoriously!" And turning to his men, the French officer shouted: *"Légionnaires! Le drapeau juif! Salut!* Legionnaires, the Jewish flag! Salute! . . . ."

"Just as soon as we start the big push," said General Montgomery, "I want to create a little diversion behind Rommel's lines. I would like to take one of his supply depots on the Libyan coast. I had thought of the town of Bardia, that is the nearest to us. I do not think we could hold it for any length of time, for the place is strongly held by an entire division of Italians who have German artillery support. But holding on to Bardia is not the first essential at the present stage of the game, although permanent seizure would, of course, be a big help. For the moment I would be satisfied with raising hell there for a few hours, blowing up the munition dumps and the petrol supply which is stored in the caves near the shore, wrecking the tank and aviation repair shops, and ruining the harbour. What do you say? Do you think it can be done?"

The words were addressed to Commander Osterman-Averni, chief of a Jewish "suicide-task force" from Palestine serving with the Eighth Army. Commander Osterman-Averni has told the story in the Hebrew daily newspaper *Hamashkif*, which is published in Jerusalem and I have verified it from other sources.

"Three days after General Montgomery called us to headquarters," he writes, "we were inside Bardia. But we did not go alone. I mean my task force was joined by another Jewish suicide commando. Together we went in. I wouldn't be surprised if the Italians of the

Bardia garrison, who are now nearly all prisoners of war, were still trying to solve the riddle of how we got there. Actually, the answer to their puzzle is extremely simple.

"We were put aboard two destroyers in the late afternoon. As usual, the men were not told in advance of their destination. They imagined that our task would be one of those routine 'behind-the-line' actions: the demolition of a bridge, the destruction of a water supply line, or some similar task. They did not have any particular reason to devote much speculative thinking to the task ahead . . . .

"When we were nearing land, I told the men that we were going to land at Bardia and that, if possible, the town was to be taken in a general assault at dawn. I told them it would not be an easy job and emphasized that strict discipline and group spirit alone could insure success. I said it was the most important task entrusted to us thus far and that the honor of the Palestinian 'suicide forces' was at stake. 'If we come through,' I said, 'I am authorized to promise each of you an additional stripe.'

" 'If the honor of the force is at stake, we will be in Bardia tomorrow morning,' spoke up a sergeant.

"We approached the Libyan shore in Stygian darkness," Commander Osterman-Averni goes on to write. "The destroyers scarcely moved as the rope ladders were let down by which we slid into the rowboats that were to set us ashore. These boats advanced stealthily. Nobody spoke. The oars barely skimmed the waters. Not a speck of light showed in Bardia. In fact, we could not even see the coast. The scraping of the boats on the rocks was the first intimation we had that we had reached our destination.

"In deepest silence we waded ashore. A patrol was sent forward immediately. We waited an hour. From the distance came the thunderous roll of our artillery. We could hear the metallic steps of the Italian sentries on the quays. When the patrol returned, reporting that they had established the exact position of the spot where we had landed, the British sailors from the warships whispered 'good luck' and dipped their oars in the water. Then we were on our own. The last contact with the Eighth Army had been broken . . . .

"We were eighty-five men in all. We had ten machine guns which required the services of twenty men. The rest of us were armed with tommy guns and knuckle-duster daggers. We had one signalman and one medical man with us.

"We advanced in the dark. Some scouts went ahead, their daggers ready for instant action. We lost all sense of time. Every minute was like an eternity. We reached the road at last, stopped, and lay down to await the report of the scouts. In this neighborhood we knew there should be an Italian guard post. Our machine guns were at the ready, to meet all eventualities. But we also knew that we must not fire yet, for it would have betrayed our presence. And that, considering that we were eighty-five men against a division, would have meant our certain annihilation.

"Forty-five minutes we waited. I was growing anxious about our scouts. Then the sound of a shrill low whistle came to us in the dark. A scout came running back. The Italian post had been taken. The scouts had carried out a 'silent job'. As we stepped up I noticed several bodies on the ground. I could not tell whether they were corpses or just stunned or tied. Nor did I care.

"Ten lorries then rumbled past over the road. They did not even dream of stopping to examine the isolated guard position. Then we advanced, the machine guns in front. Dawn was breaking. As we marched along the road into Bardia, another caravan of trucks passed by, going in the same direction as we. Our main danger was that the drivers might offer us a ride. But to our luck, all the trucks were heavily loaded, and nobody bothered with us hitchhikers. It did not seem to enter the drivers' heads that an enemy party was marching along right in their midst.

"So we kept walking until we saw our chance and made off across a field. Several blockhouses were dealt with. Their small garrisons were given 'silent treatment.' We managed to advance to a well-built concrete blockhouse. The garrison was still asleep. We quickly dispatched all of them while they lay on their cots. Then we made ourselves comfortable, set up our machine guns, and waited.

"When an hour after dawn a deafening roar heralded the artillery barrage of our own guns, indicating that the British 'push' was on, we heard the signals all around us, calling the blockhouse garrisons to the defense. Italian soldiers streamed out of them and ran forward. And we opened fire on them.

"One officer, thinking that his men were being fired on by mistake, shouted at us, but we continued to fire. After a while it dawned on the Italians that something was wrong. Two companies appeared, cautiously approaching our position. When they were quite near, we hurled a well-aimed mass of hand grenades at them. They dispersed in panic.

"Fire was opened at us by their machine guns from all directions, but it was ineffective since we were in a good position of concealment. They got their artillery to open fire on us too, but their fire was misdirected, since their own men were all over and they could not easily pick out as a special target the one blockhouse we occupied.

"But now shells of our own guns began falling dangerously near. Realizing that we were no longer an unknown quantity, we flashed signals to our own observers overhead and in the general direction of where our main forces might be. After an hour or so we knew that we had been seen, for the shells of the British artillery outside Bardia began giving our blockhouse a wide clearance.

"We then redoubled our fire on the Italian rear, and their officers, believing themselves surrounded by superior forces, hoisted white flags on the blockhouses. The town of Bardia was ours. But we did not leave our blockhouse except to occupy a few more of the neighboring pillboxes, where we manned the captured Italian machine guns. We could not very well show the enemy how few we were, for in that case he might well have regretted his surrender and turned on us. By midafternoon the first wave of British infantry and the motorized units moved into Bardia without firing a shot.

"We did not raise hell in Bardia, it is true. We did

better: we captured everything intact and nine thousand enemy prisoners to boot . . . ."

In June, 1942, when Rommel dropped that contemptuous remark about playing a mere game of cat and mouse with the British Eighth Army and the whole civilized world wondered why he delayed giving the signal that would send his Panzer divisions on what appeared in all likelihood to be their last single day's drive into the Nile Valley and to the shores of the Suez Canal, General Bernard Montgomery was as much in a quandary as anybody else. We know now that the Nazi commander was purposely biding his time, perfecting his plans to the last minute detail, collecting such enormous supplies that when the hour of attack finally struck his last dash would be one glorious, irresistible climax to the long desert campaign—an assault so powerful that British resistance would melt at the first onset and turn into an unparalleled debacle. But this was not known at British headquarters. At least, no one there could imagine the real cause of delaying the blow that might well prove fatal. Nobody knew exactly what trick Rommel had up his sleeve.

That is why General Montgomery according to an informant in the British Near Eastern Command at Cairo, wanted to know if it would not be possible for some British soldiers to dress up in German uniforms, go out into the desert, make contact with some units of the Afrika Korps, and try to ferret out the secret of Rommel's designs. A delicate job, one that required more than ordinary circumspection, tact, and courage.

If their identity was to be discovered by the Nazis, such men could not expect to be treated as mere prisoners of war. They were spies pure and simple and would inexorably meet the spy's swift death. And then: where find in the British army a group of men who could speak German so fluently that they would not be detected at the first contact with real Germans? Maybe there was a former Heidelberg student in the ranks of the Eighth Army, but of what value would one individual be on a mission like that? He would almost immediately draw attention to himself and come under suspicion, even if he should manage to enter the German lines as a free man. His usefulness would be at an end immediately.

Brigadier-General Kisch, in charge of Montgomery's supply, hearing of the project and of the search for German-speaking soldiers, told the Commander in Chief at dinner one night that he knew where to get volunteers for the job. "There are plenty of German-Jewish refugees amongst my engineers," he said, "and plenty more in the Buffs. Why don't you try them?"

Kisch's proposal was adopted. About forty German-Jewish youths from Palestine serving with the Eighth Army were examined as to fitness, perfection of language, and courage. In the end twenty were selected to go out, wander about in some section of the Western Desert ostensibly to repair barbed-wire entanglements in front of the German position and thus try to make contact with parties of Rommel's men similarly engaged, in some part of no man's land, during the lull of battle. The twenty were accordingly dressed in German engineers' uniforms, given the identity papers of fallen or captured Germans, and told to familiarize themselves with their new names. They were told to practice German military colloquialisms before setting out on their extra perilous and important venture.

Ten men and an officer disappeared into the desert and were never heard of again . . . . They must have been discovered and their real identity established almost as soon as they made contact with the Afrika Korps. The other party's fate is definitely known, for one of the ten, the officer in charge, returned. He was brought into Montgomery's presence after his harrowing experience and told the Commander in Chief: "On the fifth day out, in the neighborhood of Lahuntay we noticed a party of German engineers halting their trucks by the side of a salt depression and proceeding to lay down some road mines in a stretch of hard sand between the saline deposits and a gray mass of schist rocks that gradually rise to the west into hill-sized outcroppings of quartz. It was the only passable way for trucks and tanks for miles around, and the mines the Germans were burying were of course designed to take care of our supply columns. We worked our way unseen through the rocks and started to work on the other end of the passage about three miles away from the German party, pretending of course that we had not noticed them at all.

"An hour or so may have gone by when the Germans, having become aware of us and having spotted our German uniforms, trucks, and equipment, sent over one of their cars. We greeted them nonchalantly. But the officer asked what we were doing in that place. We told him that we had the same job as he–laying down mines–and that we had been sent out the day before by the Fifth Engineering Division of General Buchhalter's army. We gave the names of our officers, showed him our orders, and apparently satisfied him. We continued our work, planting duds. In the evening the officer of the German working party came over once more and asked us whether we intended to stay or return with him. We said we had finished our task, but that our regiment's camp was so far off that we had perhaps better stay and sleep on the spot, making the return journey in the morning, to get more mines.

"He suggested we come with him and spend the evening at his regiment's encampment, which was but fifty or sixty miles distant.

"This we accepted. We spent that night inside the German lines. We ate our meal and sat around with the men talking and smoking till eleven. One of us said that from Lahuntay as far as the eye can reach there wasn't the faintest sign of the English and that it wouldn't surprise him if the road to Alexandria were wide open. This brought on a flood of comments, of soldiers' talk, of which the general tenor was that in another ten days the advance would be under way. We made out that as soon as the last reinforcements, which had already landed at Benghazi, had joined the main army, the great assault would be launched. We asked some casual questions, giving them to understand that we knew all about the date of attack and even said that we knew to what position we would move ourselves on the appointed day. This brought replies that made it seem certain that the enemy's chief effort will not be in the coastal region but on our left flank.

They were all, it seems, going to concentrate there . . . . at least the men of the units with whom we spoke.

"The following morning we drove off after breakfast and towards noon did another stretch of work. This time a British Spitfire soared overhead, swerved around a couple of times, and gave us a good strafing. We joined a work party returning to camp and had the same experience as the night before.

"On the second morning as we stood around our only truck ready to move off with the intention of regaining our own lines that day or the next, we noticed that something was amiss. We saw a military policeman on the other side of our truck examine the hood closely, lift it up, and remove the magneto. The man then walked off.

"'Something's up,' I said to my men. 'Stand by the truck and get your guns ready. If we are trapped we'll give them a lesson. There's no use surrendering. We are spies and Jews at that. They'll give us the usual torture . . . .'

"There was no chance of making a getaway. Our truck stood in the general parking grounds of the division and was on all sides surrounded by other vehicles about to move off, hundreds of mechanics busy all around.

"I said to my men that I would go to the quartermaster's stores and see if I could get a new magneto.

"I had scarcely gone a hundred paces when the sound of firing struck my ears. I ran back, fearing that my men were in trouble. They were. They were standing in a bunch against our truck, their tommy guns in their hands, firing into a German military police detail of about fifty men who were advancing on them in a wide semicircle. From all over the camp men were running in the direction of the firing. Two of my men had clambered aboard the truck and were tossing out hand grenades with deadly effect. Germans were toppling over like nine pins. The others were firing their tommy guns point-blank into the mass of soldiers milling about. The affray did not last more than five minutes. My men's ammunition gave out, and they were massacred. But around them lay a pile of dead and wounded ten times bigger than our party. I walked out of the camp as casually as I could. On the way a German major who was walking back to his hut remarked: 'That was a helluva stunt. Those fellows were Jews from Palestine. One of our policemen, a former German colonist from Sarona, spotted them this morning as they were eating their breakfast . . . .' "

One of the Jewish colonies in Palestine, Hanita, in Galilee, against the establishment of which the Palestine administration raised heaven and earth a few years back, played an important role in the war against the Vichy regime in Syria.

It was in 1938 that the Jewish National Fund acquired several hundred dunams of land in the north western corner of Upper Galilee near the borders of Lebanon and notified the British administration of its intention to establish an agricultural colony on the newly purchased territory. A beginning was to be made with the redemption of the Galilean province of the Holy Land, once the most densely settled and most flourishing agricultural area of Palestine, now for the most part a howling wilderness of rock and treeless solitude.

The Palestine administration at once vetoed the project. The High Commissioner, Sir Harold Mac Michael, based his objection on the argument that colonists taking up residence in so remote and isolated a district would present a constant temptation to Bedouin raiders both from across and inside the borders of Palestine. The nearest Jewish habitations were in eastern Galilee, too far for their settlers to come to the aid of an establishment in western Galilee in the event of danger. If the Jews, the High Commissioner intimated, instead of starting in the extreme northern wilds of Galilee, would establish colonies in the south of that province and then gradually push northward, establishing colonies chainwise or rather like stepping-stones in the direction of the frontier, something might perhaps be said for the reclamation of Galilee. But to establish the first settlement at the extreme limit of Palestinian territory, in a godforsaken sort of no man's land, was a too hazardous enterprise for which he, Sir Harold, would not assume responsibility.

The directors of the Jewish Agency replied that they would be glad enough to establish an entire chain of colonies but that the administration's land-buying regulations had so far precluded the purchase of sites that might serve as steppingstones on the road to the north. They must therefore start where they could–that is, on the spot which had just recently become the property of the Jewish people. Sir Harold proved adamant. His interpretation of the mandate which charges Britain with facilitating "the close settlement of Jews on the land" works out in practice in placing, by order of the government of Great Britain, of course, as many obstacles in the way of the purchase of land by Jews as possible and after that, if the Jews still succeed in getting hold of a plot of barren, rocky, desert land on which no human being in his right senses would live, in discouraging them from settling on it.

Only, the Jews would not take no for an answer. They could not abide by the High Commissioner's decision. In withholding his official fiat, the High Commissioner may well have been carrying out his duty in that he acted in the spirit of those restrictive measures designed against and imposed upon Jewish Palestine by a narrow-minded, anti-Jewish bureaucracy in the sole interests not of the British Empire, but of a handful of feudalistic Arab landowners. The Palestinian Jews, on the other hand, could not do otherwise than what they did. They insisted again and again that the High Commissioner's decision be revoked and that the colony be opened up—that particular colony and others, always more colonies and settlements by hook or by crook. For the Palestinian Jews feel behind their backs the ever-growing anguish and desperate pressure of the homeless and hopeless Jewish masses in Europe still seeking a way out of what had become to millions of them a gruesome deathtrap or a living hell after Hitler's advent to power . . . .

After months of wearisome palaver, pleading and insisting on the one side, haggling and quibbling on the other, with references to the Colonial Office in London going to and fro, the High Commissioner finally, reluctantly gave in. The Jews were permitted to establish that colony on their own land in their own country. They could go out there to that desolate spot in Galilee if they wanted to, but they must not blame the administration if disaster should overtake them on the pioneer trail.

"*Mi yivne ha-Galil?* Who will build Galilee?" the young people sang that night all over Palestine, when the government's decision became known.

"*El yivne ha-Galil!* God will build Galilee!" came the answering chorus.

The tract of four thousand dunams had been thoroughly explored and surveyed in the meantime. It would provide a living for eighty families, or five hundred souls, if they could engage in mixed farming: sheep raising and poultry breeding, with tobacco the chief crop. All this had been settled by the agronomical experts who had examined the land. One third of the area was to be used for pasturage, and one of the first tasks of the settlers would be the planting of a forest of eucalyptus trees. For deforestation and consequent soil erosion constitute one of the worst blights of the Holy Land. The candidates to take up the work were in readiness, too. The occupation group consisted of ninety young people, eighty men and ten women. They were to go out before the bulk of the settlers and make the place fit for habitation. The pioneers had been carefully selected from many localities with reference to their fitness and courage for occupying a new tract in a frontier region where only recently fierce battles had raged between government forces and Arab bands.

The occupation took place in what has become of

late years the usual form for establishing new settlement in Palestine: the colony was completed in all essentials between sunrise and sunset in one single day. All preliminary preparations were made in the workers' quarter in Emek Zebulon, at the foot of Mount Carmel. The caravan of trucks was on the way while the moon still hung over the dark waters of the Mediterranean. Thirty-seven lorries loaded with tents, planks, mattresses, cots, length of iron pipes, provisions, and water rumbled off into the future. The orders were that they must stay closely together, that there was to be no singing on the road, and that no one change from one truck to another. At the head of the procession rode a party of ghafirs, or supernumerary constables, themselves Jewish pioneers. Behind them, in motorcars, were four hundred laborers, who were to return in the evening after the colony was established At the tail end, behind the trucks, trotted a contingent of donkeys needed to carry loads up the hill. A second group of ghafirs brought up the rear.

The sun came up as the party arrived on the chosen spot. Immediately the workers scattered to tasks previously assigned to them. Some began to mark out the by-road which was to connect the settlement with the Haifa-Beyrouth highway running along the Mediterranean shore, less than a mile distant. Two springs had been discovered by the surveyors. Their waters were now brought to the camp by means of pipes. Tents were pitched, weeds uprooted, stones pried loose for a barricade behind a barbed-wire fence which was going up in the meantime. The high wooden watchtower was set in place with a giant searchlight. Some of the ghafirs stood on guard while the rest hammered and shoveled and got to work, although their rifles remained near by for handy reference, if need be . . . .

At midday a recess is called. The food is quickly eaten, for there is still much to be done before nightfall. But a few minutes remain before the back-to-work signal will be given, and someone starts to sing *"Alinu hartza*, we have gone up to the land!" Instantly the Hora dance circles form, widen, expand, whirl like wheels within wheels, faster and faster. But not for long . . . .

"La avoda, back to work!" Hammers pound, saws buzz and rip, picks clang their way into strong ground. All hands are working at top speed. There is not a minute to lose. The settlement must be completed before nightfall, and sun has now passed the meridian. A fresh breeze comes up from the Mediterranean. It must be near five o'clock, the hour when the old-world sea always stirs mysteriously, no matter how calm the weather.

But then there is an interruption. A delegation has come to the newest settlement in western Galilee from the oldest in eastern Galilee, bringing a gift of a Sefer Torah, a scroll of the Law. All work comes to a standstill. Quickly a tent is cleared out and converted into a synagogue. Six young men advance and in turn kiss the scroll which is contained in a cylindrical velvet-covered, tubelike box with a ring of little silver bells fastened to the top of its axis. The whole company forms a procession to take the Word of God to its new home.

All at once the man bearing the scroll breaks into singing: *"El bene, bene betcha belzarov*, build thy house, O God, build it speedily!" The congregation takes up the prayerful chant, and they dance as long ago their king, the "man after God's own heart," once danced when the Ark of the Covenant was brought to Jerusalem.

"I was glad," shouts one man, with arms outstretched and dancing about, "I was glad when they said unto me: let us go into the house of the Lord!" All the colonists repeat the words of the One Hundred and Twenty-second Psalm: "Pray for the peace of Jerusalem: they shall prosper that love thee . . . ."

Now the sun is going down swiftly. The visitors and helpers from Haifa are leaving. Most of the ghafirs are piling into their cars. That night five troopers will remain behind with the ninety young men and women in the wilderness. Darkness gathers quickly in the Holy Land. The colonists are in their new home, for better or for worse . . . .

For worse, it seems! At midnight the colony is attacked by a large guerrilla band. The prowlers are spotted by the revolving searchlight when they are only two hundred yards distant and in the act of dividing themselves into three columns for the assault on the colony. The watchmen shout the alarm. Instantly the night is filled with the warcry of the Bedouin. It comes from all sides. The attacking force must be a thousand strong. The searchlight beats down on the white-cloaked figures now running at top speed. They are coming from three sides and firing their rifles. But the Jews have manned the barricades. They are holding their fire. Suddenly the searchlight goes out. The attackers are too near now to let the light burn: it would give away the position of the defenders. The Bedouin blaze away aimlessly. But now there are short spurts of flame from the rocks of the barricade: the Jews have held their fire till their targets are unmistakably clear. Two, three, four salvos—and then stillness.

The searchlight goes on and slowly turns its beam on the surrounding country: the Bedouin are streaming back. The firing has stopped altogether. Nothing is heard but the moaning and whimpering of the wounded. The beam points fiercely at a fallen Bedouin who is trying to raise himself on one hand while keeping the other convulsively clamped over his abdomen. When he becomes aware that the light keeps him in focus, he turns his face in the direction of the camp and cries out in a whimpering voice: "Don't kill me, *baba!* Don't kill me, I am your brother!" The light moves abruptly away from him. It sweeps, without stopping, over what appear mere bundles of white rags and then peers into the distance, lighting up the bluish hills opposite.

The Bedouin are assembling for a new assault. The three columns are now merging into one solid phalanx. There is to be a mass attack this time. It is to come from the north side of the colony, the side where the barricade has not been completed. The first attackers have discovered the colony's weak spot. They now come running forward en masse, filling the night with their unearthly screeching. The searchlight beats down on them. When they are four hundred yards away they drop to the ground and begin to disperse, crawling on hands and knees, taking advantage of every clump of shrubbery and of every boulder. Whenever the search-

[215]

light is turned in a southerly direction for a moment, to see that no enemies are sneaking up from the rear, the attackers in front, taking advantage of the temporary darkness, dash forward a few yards. The whole plain is filled with creeping, crawling figures.

At a shout from one of the leaders they get to their feet and rush for the opening in the fence. The first men are fifty yards away when once more they drop to the ground. Now they fire their guns. The searchlight is bespattered with bullets. In a flash the Bedouin are up and running again. They are only twenty yards off. Their faces can be clearly distinguished. Many carry a knife between their teeth. That will be for throat-cutting and mutilation when they get within the colony. But now with a simultaneous crash the colonists' rifles spit fire. The foremost ranks of the attackers go down with a terrifying shout, the second and third waves push on over the bodies of the fallen. Another salvo from the colony, as deadly as the first. It is immediately followed by a third and a fourth. The Jewish fire is sustained. Some Bedouin are right on top of the barbed-wire fence. One of them shouts to his followers: "We are in!" as he flourishes a long knife. At the same moment he grabs his throat and falls. A Jewish girl has shot him through the mouth. The bodies of three or four of his immediate followers fall on top of him, a writhing cluster of wounded and dead.

The others still out in the field begin to waver. They fire their rifles and run back; first, individuals only, then the entire band turns and flees. The Jewish fire keeps up relentlessly. Every shot finds its mark among the retreating guerrillas. Dozens of white-cloaked figures slump forward. They do not rise again. Soon the night is still, except for the cry of wounded men.

Once more, just before dawn, the horde returns. But again it is bloodily repulsed. When a British police patrol arrives at seven o'clock, the colonists are watering the donkeys and rigging up the rest of the barricade. Others are busy putting the roof over the tool shed.

"What happened here last night?" asks the officer commanding the patrol.

"We were attacked!" replies one of the colonists.

"That's rather obvious," says the officer. "The whole plain is covered with dead men. We surprised the last Bedouin carrying off their wounded . . . . Have you any casualties?"

The colonist points in the direction of the tent where the scroll of the Law was placed the previous afternoon. "Eight dead, one wounded; he is dying too!"

"Well, this is no place for a colony anyway," says the officer shaking his head. "What will you do if they come back tonight?"

"We will be ready for them!" says the Jew quietly, as he drives a stake into the ground.

The officer looks into the tent where the dead lie and takes out a notebook. He writes something down in it, walks out, swings back into the saddle, and rides off with his men.

Thus ends the first day in the life of Hanita, the name by which the colony is to be known. Hanita means *spearhead,* a pointing arrow.

The Bedouin do not come back the next day or the night after that. Before a week is over the colonists have built a blockhouse from the boulders gathered from the land. It stands in the middle of the colony like a citadel. It houses the administrative office and the hospital, but it can also hold the entire colony's population of four hundred souls if they are attacked again. But the rest of the year 1938 goes by, and 1939 too, and no attack comes. The schoolhouse has been built; stables, the little synagogue, and the storage shed also rise. The first crop has been harvested. Hanita grows: a park has been laid out, and a theatrical company has been giving performances for a week. The trees in the eucalyptus forest come to the height of a man's chest. Another colony has just been started at a distance of three miles. The year 1940 has just dawned . . . .

A British patrol rides up one day. The officer dismounts and enters the offices in the citadel. He wants to speak to the colonists. The men gather around him. He speaks bluntly and to the point. "Have you men sufficient knowledge of the trails leading into the Lebanon country to guide the Australian troops? There is going to be an attack on Syria. The Vichy French are letting German 'tourists' into the territory of the Syrian Republic . . . . They are laying out airdromes for the Luftwaffe . . . . Dozens of German transport planes are coming in daily across the border with men and equipment . . . . Britain has not declared war on Vichy yet. But Britain cannot tolerate the attitude of the Vichyites much longer. She cannot permit a German army near the Mosul oil fields and the Suez Canal. Australian troops are moving up from the south now. There is going to be an invasion of Syria. The High Commissioner wants to know whether the men of

Hanita are willing to serve as guides . . . ."

The High Commissioner! Sir Harold has apparently forgotten the long squabble he had over the establishment of the colony. Hanita is going to be a base for the Australians attacking Syria . . . .

Two days before British forces, in collaboration with the Free French, invaded Syria, fifty young Jews from the colony of Hanita struck out across country, entered the territory of the Lebanese Republic, avoiding all Vichyite frontier posts and patrols. After a march of seventeen hours, they halted in sight of Fort Gouraud. This stronghold, which is built on the site of an ancient Crusaders' castle in the foothills of the Lebanon range, dominates for a space of ten miles the hard, sandy highway running between Haifa and Acre, in Palestine, and Tyre, Sidon, and Beyrouth, in Syria. The road is flanked on the west by the Mediterranean whose waters it skirts, and on the east by sand dunes and the steep rocky crags of the Lebanon chain. Within range of Fort Gouraud's guns lie three bridges, two to the south and one to the north. These bridges, which form part of the coastal highway, link the steep banks of three swift mountain torrents which, descending from the Lebanon, throw themselves over a series of cataracts and rapids into the sea.

The Jews of Hanita had been asked by the British military command, because of their familiarity with the wild and unchartered Galilean-Lebanese border country, to take up a position in the neighbourhood of Fort Gouraud and, if possible, to prevent the three bridges from being destroyed by the Vichy French. For

[219]

it was along the Acre-Beyrouth highway and its three bridges that the invasion's Australian spearhead was to advance into Syria. The destruction of the bridges would naturally hold up the invasion and might in fact well turn it into disaster, as it would mean leaving baggage, trucks, artillery, and tanks behind. Fort Gouraud, moreover, is so placed that a column of troops marching north along the Beyrouth highway can be taken under the fire of its guns long before any effective reply can be given.

The task allotted to the Jews was therefore not only difficult but also extremely hazardous and, one may well add, foolhardy in the extreme. Everything depended on seizing the bridges by surprise and holding them, under the fire of Fort Gouraud's guns, until the Australians should come up in force along the highway. But the British command knew well what it was doing when it chose the Jews from Hanita for this risky undertaking. The leader of the Jewish francs-tireurs, Moshe Dayan, and ten of his companions had just been liberated from prison in Acre, where they were serving life sentences for . . . . having explored the Lebanese border region and for having engaged in scouting activities in connection with the defence of their colony. Nearly all the Jewish scouts who served the invading British and French forces in the invasion of Syria—that is, the guides of the seven spearheads—were Jews released from jail where they were serving long terms for having prepared themselves for the precise task they were now called upon to carry out. They called to mind that simple and heroic man Raziel,* the com-

---

*That Day Alone, Garden City Press, New York, 1943.

mander of the secret Jewish defense force, who was taken from jail by General Wavell's order to go into Iraq at the time of the Rashid Ali revolt against Britain and keep the Arab allies of Hitler from destroying the invaluable oil refineries of Mosul . . . .

Having come in sight of Fort Gouraud, Moshe Dayan and his men first explored the neighbourhood. They noticed that although the Vichyites guarded the bridges but weakly, on the ramparts of the fort, a thousand yards off, there was a row of machine guns pointing their nozzles in the direction of the bridges, which would make it most difficult if not to seize them, at least to hold them for any length of time. They therefore decided to take the fort itself and thus make themselves master of the position that controlled the entire district. This was easier said than done. There was a garrison of three hundred tough Somali troops in Fort Gouraud and although many of these were periodically absent on patrolling and reconnoitering duty in the neighborhood and on guard at certain strategic points, there remained a good hundred men within the walls of the fort within easy call of the ramparts with their artillery and machine guns. All the arms the Jews had were ten tommy guns.

Nevertheless, they would take the chance. There seemed no alternative. The Australian column, they knew, had left Haifa and would presently move headlong into the range of Fort Gouraud's guns, for the highway was exposed to the view of the Vichyite sentries and lookouts for a distance of five miles on either side. The Somalis could make all the preparations to have the Australians walk into a first-class deadly ambush.

[221]

This must not be! Moshe Dayan and his men therefore, crawled up to the fort's gate at the crack of dawn,
knocked the sentries over, overpowered the guard, and
raced for the ramparts. There they seized the machine
guns, swung them around, and pointed them in the
direction of the small parade ground between the
barrack buildings. As they busied themselves on the
ramparts a few shots were fired at them from the windows of the brick barracks, but when the Jews let the
machine guns talk back and sent a few squirts of bullets into the building the Somalis came out with up-
raised hands and surrendered.

The Vichyites were then ordered to pile up their
rifles and small arms in the square and to remain in-
doors. Fort Gouraud was taken. And Dayan hoisted
the Union Jack as a signal to the Australians when they
should come in sight that all was well. This was an
error. For the Somali outposts guarding the bridges,
having heard the sound of machine gun fire inside the
fort and now seeing the British flag aloft over the main
building, promptly set off one of the prepared charges
under the southernmost bridge. With a deafening roar
and clanking of steel and in a cloud of smoke, the
girders collapsed. Dayan, realizing that he had been
outwitted, immediately took the other two bridges
under fire and thus prevented the Vichyites from crippling them in turn. He intended to keep up his fire
till the Australians should arrive.

However, he had not noticed that some of the prisoners locked up in the barracks had had an opportunity
to escape by a door in the cellar. These men had
joined their comrades' patrols outside the fort and

informed them that the enemy was a mere handful of nonprofessional soldiers and that a joint effort could not fail to expel the bold intruders. By noon all the Vichy patrols in the neighborhood had been assembled, several hundred men in all, and were making ready to take the fort back.

They began by crawling through the shrubbery and picking off the Jews on the ramparts one by one. In a short time Dayan's force was reduced by seven men, more or less seriously wounded by the Somali sharpshooters. Then the attackers reentered the fort through the same cellar door through which the prisoners had escaped a few hours earlier. They rushed upstairs into the barrack building, mounted machine guns they had brought along, and took the ramparts under fire from the rear. Dayan now was compelled to switch his own guns around in order to defend himself. Five more of his men fell. But now the Somalis were fixing bayonets, and their snipers were taking up advantageous positions in the square, on the roofs of buildings, and in the stock rooms of the arsenal. A hail of bullets whizzed about the heads of the Jews on the walls. Once, twice, a concerted bayonet attack was beaten off, but each cost Dayan ten of his men. It was obvious that he could not hold out and that sooner or later he would be overwhelmed and annihilated. In desperation he planned to make a sortie, get out of the fort, rush for the bridges, and hold them perhaps another hour, two at the most, until the Australians should finally come up. But the sustained fire from the barracks windows made the idea of leaving impossible. Once more he trained his field glasses on the highway. It was getting dark. The ammunition was running out. The Somalis were coming nearer and nearer. Only twenty-two of his men were able to stand up. Another hour, nay less, and then the end would be there. But then, yes, there six or seven miles away was a cloud of dust. "They are here!" shouted Dayan. As he spoke a bullet struck his field glasses and drove the instrument into his eye. He tore it out and the eye with it.

At the same moment the Somalis launched another attack with the bayonet and with hand grenades. This time they reached the ramparts and actually got on the walls. The Jews fought them off in a hand-to-hand encounter, with knives, with bricks loosened from the walls, with crowbars and revolvers. As they were forced into a corner, two Very lights, first a red one, then a white bulb hanging in the sky beneath its floating parachute, flew overhead. The Australians had surmised what was going on in the fort and had sent up the signals. At once the French surrendered a second time. It was high time. Dayan's men had thrown their last grenade. They were fighting with their bare hands. They had held off the enemy for seven hours and resisted ten mass attacks. In the night the bridge was repaired, and the invasion of Syria by British regulars was on its way.

That's Moshe Dayan, incidentally, the man with the black bandage over his left eye who runs the gasoline station in Colony Hanita–Colony Spearhead–these days . . . .

There was a Jewish battalion among the defenders

[224]

of Tobruk during the long siege . . . .

It was Major Richard Perach, a Jew from Talpiot, who led the battalion which turned the flank of the famous Mareth Line . . . .

Jewish suicide-task forces landed in Tobruk and helped capture the city as they had captured Bardia earlier . . . .

It was General Frederick Kisch, a Jew from Haifa, who organized and supervised the immense undertaking of Montgomery's supply in the battles of Egypt and on the 1300-mile trek through Libya and Cyrenaica right to the gates of Bizerte, where he was killed . . . .

Jewish engineers organized and manned the coastal defense and signal services of Lebanon, Palestine, Sinai, and the Red Sea coast.

Entire Jewish families in Palestine enlisted in the British service—fathers and sons, mothers and daughters—in the medical corps and the Red Cross.

The Jewish coast guard ran one hundred speed boats along the dangerous Mediterranean lines between Cyprus, Palestine, Egypt, and Libya . . . .

Two thousand-five hundred Palestinian Jews served with the Royal Air Force as bombardiers, pilots, and observers. Six thousand more Jews were in the ground crews of the Egyptian airdromes . . . .

Jewish engineers constructed Montgomery's impregnable forts at El Alamein . . . .

All the antiaircraft stations in the Holy Land were manned by Palestinian Jews . . . .

Jewish units took a leading part in the capture of Sidi Barrani, Sollum, and Fort Capuzzo and were praised by General Sir Archibald Wavell for "their courage and self-sacrifice" in those engagements.

Jewish "suicide squads," especially chosen for their toughness, daring, and mobility, fought in Eritrea and Ethiopia.

"On reaching the Mogarreh Valley the Palestinians," one dispatch to G.H.Q. reported, "had the task of covering the left flank of the advance on Keren, and the cutting off of the Italians on a ridge to the left of the main attacking force. They thus helped to take 2500 prisoners and bring to a successful conclusion an extremely tough and courageous action."

A Jew, Shmaryahu Weinstein, was the hero of the battle of Keren, in Abyssinia: he saved a whole company of South Africans by sacrificing his own life.

Thirty Jews were killed in the Amba-Algai area in Ethiopia when they, forming a suicide-task force, rushed forward to capture a hill that bristled with the machine guns of the Duke of Aosta's forces.

Jewish units—suicide-task forces—penetrated and demolished enemy fortifications night after night during the campaign in Abyssinia. Peter Fraser, Prime Minister of New Zealand, said that his country and Australia were proud of the way the Palestinian Jews stood shoulder to shoulder with New Zealanders and Australians in "the hottest engagements" in Greece, Crete and Erithrea.

Jewish engineers, the Jewish Pioneer Corps, and Jewish pilots fought in Greece. Their services and severe losses were recognized by Sir Henry Maitland Wilson, the commanding officer in Palestine.

Three thousand Jews, residents of Palestine, joined the national armies of the countries to which they owed allegiance—Czechoslovakia, Holland, France, Poland . . . .

It took the war and, above all, Marshal Rommel's grave and long-lasting threat to inter-Empire and inter-Allied lines of communication to set in strong relief the value of the settlement of half a million Jews in Palestine–that is to say, in the immediate vicinity of the most vital arteries of the British world system. Jewish Palestine contributed more effectively to the repulse of the Axis advance upon Syria, Iraq, Egypt, and the Suez Canal, to the triumph of British arms in Ethiopia, Eritrea, and Somaliland, and to the final liberation of the Libyan and Tripolitanian coastal regions than the fifty times larger populations of the Arab countries combined.

In all that Eastern world where hazardous contingencies lurked around every corner or lay carelessly strewn about as so much explosive, the Jews were the only ones who took their stand at Britain's side without hesitation or flinching. They responded to the call to the full measure of their ability. They did more: they responded before a call was made. No more than the Arabs of Egypt, Iraq, or Trans-Jordan were the Palestinian Jews, by reason of some existing tie of allegiance or loyalty, bound to espouse the British cause. They were neither British subjects nor nationals of one of the United Nations allied with Great Britain. They were merely inhabitants of a territory which is temporarily administered. Nothing could be expected of them beyond compliance with the general laws in vogue. According to international law, Palestine is a neutral country, and its inhabitants are neutrals.

It is true that the Palestinian Jews could not have acted otherwise than they did whatever their legal position, inasmuch the moral issues involved in the war determined their choice. Like the prophets of old, the Palestinian Jewish community measured its duty by the objective morality and not by its own intrinsic interests. What were they to gain in allowing the best of the limited Jewish man power in Palestine to throw itself into battle when there did not exist a guarantee, or even the prospect of a guarantee, that Britain would permit a replacement of the inevitable losses by a greater volume of immigration than that stipulated by the White Paper of 1939. The Palestinian Jews were under no illusion, when they placed their lives, their wealth, and their honor at the disposal of Great Britain, that the gesture would be graciously returned with at least a promise of the discontinuation of the destructive policy pursued by the British Colonial Office in the building of the Jewish national home. In their case truly the only recompense was blood, sweat, and tears. Even hope, which is the most puissant incentive of the other peoples engaged in the struggle for liberation, was denied them.

It may be objected, of course, that the contribution of so small a country as Palestine with a population numerically insignificant when measured against the fantastic number of human beings involved in the war cannot have been of decisive import. It may also be argued that it is too much to believe that the Jews were motivated entirely by a sentiment of altruism when they sprang to the Empire's defense. But to this the reply must be made that when a sensitive pair of scales is evenly balanced, the smallest straw will upset the equilibrium. Jewish Palestine was that straw. The forces engaged on either side in the Near East were not at all commensurate with the gigantic scope of the world struggle. Rommel, who represented the chief menace, never had more than 200,000 men under his command in Africa. Until Montgomery took over from Auchenleck, the British, Mr. Churchill has declared, had at no time more than 45,000 men on the African front. Of these 45,000 a quarter were Jews.

Not until the joint Anglo-American landing in Morocco and Algeria did the British have more men and material in the North African-Near Eastern theater of war than their German adversary. But by this time the scene of battle had shifted thirteen hundred miles away from the Egyptian border. Tunisia is not in the Near East. The battle for Egypt and the Suez Canal was won by Bernard Montgomery before American troops set foot on Africa's shore. It was the British Eighth Army that turned the tide. In that army and supporting that army were thirty thousand Jewish volunteers and two hundred thousand Palestinian industrial workers and farmers. In the circumstances that was not a negligeable force.

As to the basic motive of the Palestinian Jews in throwing their lot with the British Empire: the deed itself is not supremely significant; decisive are the intention and the soul of the doer. What counts is not what is done, but how it is done. The Jews of Palestine collaborated instinctively, spontaneously, and wholeheartedly. Renan once said: "That which causes men to

form a people is not only the recollection of great things
they have done together, but the longing and the will
to do new things."

Intuitively, the Jews of Palestine responded to a
moral challenge, to a call, to the ache of national community and common destiny a thousand years old,
thwarted and vitiated ever so long in the Diaspora and
now suddenly again become vivid, clear, and alive when
confronted by a common task. Without words or
phrases, but by the spontaneity of life, they vindicated
the fundamental tenet of the philosophy of Zionism
that through being rooted in their own land they had
become again what they always were, but now in sight
of all the world: a people, a nation, Israel reborn . . . .

In the fateful hour when Britain's fate hung in the
balance and when Rommel boasted that as far as he
was concerned it was all over but the shouting, the
little land of Palestine placed at the disposal of the
British Empire and its armies in the Near East an industrial apparatus of seven thousand factories, large
and small.

It may sound fantastic, but it must be said, for it is
the truth: nobody, neither the British High Command
nor Marshal Rommel, had counted on Palestine to
play the role it did in that battle which decided–future
chroniclers will declare–the world's destiny. Of course,
everybody knew that Palestine existed and what its
resources were. But it was not realized what Palestine
meant: a powerful instrument of victory in the hands
of that Jewish community, which threw itself into the
struggle with a wholeheartedness and zeal that mul-

tiplied the country's industrial effectiveness a hundred-fold. It was the spirit that counted.

The pioneers of Palestine showed the British government, which had treated them most ungenerously, that they had not only exploited the poor natural resources of the Holy Land to the utmost, but that they had succeeded in creating new resources which had not been available twenty-five years earlier when modern Zionism launched its program of redeeming the land of Israel. Sandy wastes had been planted and cleverly cultivated. Desert solitude and grim rocks had been transformed into vineyards and orange groves. Swamps and malaria-infested regions, twenty-five years ago pestilential deathtraps for the Turkish and British armies engaged in the battles of Gaza and Megiddo, had been turned into healthy and productive areas. Wells had been dug so that no intricate and endless system of pipes had to be constructed across the Sinaian desert as when Allenby's campaign was held up by the lack of water. The rivers Jordan and Yarmuk had been electrified, the latent wealth of the Dead Sea made productive, and the godforsaken wilderness transformed into a garden fit for human habitation. As if guided by a providential foresight, the Jews had constructed a system of roads, as good as and better than Mussolini's famous *autostradi* in Libya, branching out and radiating in a hundred directions and leading up, in several critical instances, to the very borders of adjoining countries that were directly and most gravely menaced by the enemy on different occasions in the course of the present war.

The world will learn some day—and should remem-

ber at the peace conference–how certain Arab chief-
tains in Iraq, Egypt, and Saudi Arabia, who proclaimed
themselves the loyal allies of Britain and of the United
States after Rommel was beaten at the gates of Alexandria, comported themselves when Montgomery
himself said privately that only a miracle could save
him . . . .

Jewish Palestine was part of that miracle. Jewish
Palestine was one of the imponderables that turned the
tide against Hitler at the moment when he and almost
the whole world least expected it.

Besides the thirty odd thousand Jews who were
taken into the Eighth British Army and into the Palestinian home-guard forces, Jewish industries large and
small alike and Jewish agriculture in Palestine supplied
the British armies with bandages, pharmaceutical articles, ether, sulfanilamide, benzoic acid, nicotinic acid,
vitamin B complex, ascorbic acid (vitamin C), insulin,
alkaloids, microscopic stains; further: precision instruments (many of the experts of the Carl Zeiss works
of Jena, having transferred to the Holy Land a few
years previously), tobacco, 135,000 pairs of boots per
month, fruit, vegetables, wheat, wine, X-ray apparatus,
25,000 tons of cement per month, soap, chocolate, spare
parts for automobiles and trucks, sandbags, timber,
tents, linen uniforms, and buses taken from the Palestinian transportation system.

The Concrete Shipbuilding Company, organized
by a refugee shipwright from Serbia, launched a fleet
of twenty fishing trawlers, of 110 tons each, equipped
with Diesel engines also manufactured in Palestine.
The concrete manufactured by the refugee builder is

seven hundred per cent more watertight than ordinary concrete and can withstand a pressure of five hundred kilograms per square centimeter. These vessels are built in one quarter the time required for steel vessels, and the construction cost is forty per cent less. In the beginning of 1943 the company was going in for mass production of concrete barges, tankers, launches, and cargo vessels.

During the war new items and new techniques of manufacture were introduced in Palestine in turning out hydrogenated vegetable oil for the manufacture of margarine, glycerin, yeast, starch, glucose, waterproofing material, castor-oil processing for lubrication of airplane motors, and rubber hose. Ethylene gas and ethylene chlorohydrin were turned out for ripening and preserving certain crops. A new distillery was opened during the war to manufacture alcohol from carob pulp. The gum manufactured from carob seed is exported to the United States.

In 1942 nearly two million cases of waste citrus fruits were utilized for the production of pectin, alcohol, essential oil, citric acid, jams, jellies, marmalade, and dried cattle fodder.

With that Palestine sent out to the Eighth Army: laboratory equipment, electrical appliances, meat, especially mutton; photographic material, water pipes, stationery, typewriters, burr drills, steel helmets, three million dollars' worth of processed diamonds for cutting tools, beer from Palestine's two new breweries, matches from Emek Zebulon, glassware and crockery, bedding, mattresses, maps, sheet metal, parachutes, disinfectants, oil burners, armoured cars, cranes, five hundred ambulances, wire, shovels, water pails, cutlery, hammers, saws, nails, screws, saddles, camels, mules, horses, and railway equipment and steel from the Vulcan Foundry and Forge Works at Emek Zebulon.

All that material and equipment, as necessary to an army as bullets and bread, did not need to be transported through submarine-infested oceans. It was there, on the spot, at the moment it was needed most.

Palestinian Jews lugged the oil and gasoline from Haifa and Mosul across the Syrian and the Sinaian deserts to Montgomery's mechanized forces.

Palestine furnished to the British armies in Libya, Eritrea, Ethiopia, and Somaliland, thousands of doctors, nurses, and dentists. It placed the great Hadassah Medical Centre in Jerusalem at the disposal of the Empire.

The Meteorological Department of the Hebrew University prepared weather data for the British and Allied air forces operating in the whole Near and Middle East, in the Caucasus, the Sudan, Ethiopia, and Eritrea. The Hebrew University's Department of Parasitology conducted courses in war surgery and tropical medicine for the Australian Expeditionary Force. It supplied antitetanus serum and typhus serum to the Army Medical Corps and shipped 70,000 phials to the Polish army in Russia and as many phials of typhus serum to the Red Army. The Department of Oriental Studies furnished the intelligence service with interpreters familiar with all the languages and dialects of the neighborhood, including Somali, Amharic, and Galla for Ethiopia, Kurdish, Chaldean, Turkish, and Armenian for northern Iraq, and Coptic and Berber for northern Africa.

Palestine supplied the Turkish army with half a million pairs of boots and all the pharmaceutical articles and precision instruments Ankara required. To the Soviet Union went large shipments of bromine compounds, indispensible in the manufacture of explosives, a gift from the Palestine Potash Company, which exploits the resources of the Dead Sea.

Palestinian Jewry spent the equivalent of about ten million dollars to mobilize fresh resources for agricultural and industrial developments in the first two years of the war. It started twenty-five new agricultural settlements in the same years. It completed seventeen hundred new electrical power installations in the southern districts of the country alone.

For so remarkable and telling a show of devotion to the democratic cause and for so heroic and loyal, although unostentatiously rendered a performance of service to the British Empire in the darkest hour of its history, the least that could be expected from the British government even at this late date, one would think, is a public recognition of Jewish valor and an acknowledgement of Palestinian Jewry's share in that momentous victory which frustrated Germany's plan to break through to the sources of raw materials in Africa and Asia and link up with the Japanese.

Wendell Willkie said while on a visit to the Holy Land that the measure of freedom to be gained by the peoples of the Near East in the postwar era—and the Jews are one of these peoples—will depend on what contribution they made in the actual waging of the war. Willkie said that; not Churchill or Eden or Lord Cranborne, the Colonial Secretary. These men were silent. The British press was silent. Not a single British, or American newspaper for that matter, gave its readers the merest inkling of the material and strategic importance of Palestine and the role it played in the furious battle for the domination of the African and Asian markets that raged for the better part of two years in the Libyan desert.

Never once was Jewish heroism mentioned. Not a word leaked out of that numerically small Jewish community standing there like a rock in the smoldering hostile Arab world at the back of the British army. As little as possible was said of Jewish soldiers standing side by side with Englishmen, Australians, and South Africans and facing the fearful odds presented by Rommel's overwhelming superiority. And yet the Near East swarmed with foreign correspondents from the beginning of the campaign to the end.

Palestine Jewry's effort in the war must be considered the best-guarded military secret of all!

1943 BOOK REVIEWS OF
THE FORGOTTEN ALLY

by Ray McPartlin, *p17, Boston Globe, Oct. 27, 1943*

"'The Forgotten Ally' must be 1943's angriest book ... The author makes no secret of the fact that, though he is not a Jew, but a member of the Dutch Reformed Church, he appears here in the role of a prosecutor pressing to prove the counts of a sensational indictment. Readers will be aroused by his book and its style, some to wrath that matches his own, others to hot-headed disagreement, with what he has to say. But both sides need to read 'The Forgotten Ally.' Its subject is one that challenges all thoughtful people and the facts that it discloses for the first time deserve hearing."

---

by Edgar Ansel Mowrer, *Weekly Book Review, p6, Oct. 31, 1943*

"This extremely well written book by the much traveled and imaginative Mr. Van Paassen is really a disturbing accusation. **The "forgotten ally" is the Zionist Jew of Palestine.** The author accuses the United Nations in general of forgetting the Jews, and Great Britain in particular of betraying them ... To make his case, Mr. Van Paassen, with the flourishes of Luther tacking his immortal thesis to the church door at Wittenberg, makes a number of bold, challenging statements ...... **Palestinian Jews, as soldiers, engineers, workers, played a major role in the salvation of Egypt and enabled Montgomery to throw back Rommel.** Examples: A Jewish engineer built the vital bridge across the Euphrates River; a battalion of mine-laying Jewish engineers under Major Felix Liebmann held Mechli for two days against all manner of Axis assaults until relieved by French General Koenig of Bir-Hacheim fame; Jewish suicide task forces frequently went into Rommel's camp disguised as Germans. Jews helped the United Nations take Vichy-French Syria; a Jewish battalion under Major Richard Perach led the battalion that turned the Mareth line. When Montgomery took over from Auchinleck, the Egyptian Army consisted of 45,000 men. A full quarter were Jews. In the British 8th Army at one time or another were 30,000 Jewish fighters supported by (from Palestine) 200,000 "Palestinian" (read Jewish) farmers and workers (7,000 factories)...... **Of all these important Jewish contributions, no official British mention was ever made. It was the 'best kept secret of the war'."**

(Emphases added)

---

by Reinhold Niebuhr, *The Nation, Dec 25, 1943*

"...van Paassen. His sense of justice is all-embracing, so that he serves many a cause ... His most recent book was inevitable, for van Paassen has been, for a long time, the most effective Gentile champion of the Zionist answer to the Jewish problem. In this book he brings all his polemical skill to bear upon this issue ... **He advances a central thesis. It is that Britain, and to a lesser extent the allies of Britain, are appeasing an essentially unreliable Arab world while betraying the absolute loyalty of the Jewish community in Palestine** ... He makes a convincing case for his main thesis. Britain is tender with its dubious allies, precisely because they are dubious, and also because they are involved in its Indian dilemma through the Mohammedanism which partially unites the Arab with the Indian world. The Jews are unable to bargain as the Arabs do, just because they have no alternative ...." (Emphasis added)

---

by Bertha E. Josephson, *p521, American Historical Review, v.49, 1943-44*

".....His 'Best Kept Secret of the War' is a chapter well worth reading for its factual data on the important part Palestinian Jewry has played in the recent battle for Africa."

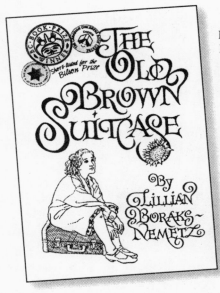

ALSO FROM BEN-SIMON PUBLICATIONS:

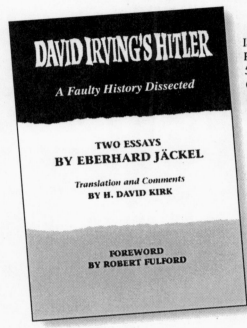

David Irving, the notorious darling of the international neo-Nazi movement, has argued in his book *Hitler's War* that Hitler did not know or approve of the destruction of the Jews of Europe. The German historian Eberhard Jäckel here shows that thesis to be false and dangerous, for it is designed to clean up Hitlers's murderous image.

"Eberhard Jäckel's article is an important contribution in the ongoing battle against Holocaust deniers. It deserves the widest possible distribution." **—Rabbi W. Gunther Plaut,**
Senior Scholar, Holy Blossom Temple, Toronto

"Dr. Jäckel has done what David Irving dares not do: apply the historian's critical scalpel to the largest single body of original evidence ever preserved from any régime in the world. The result is a stunning exposé of what Hitler knew and Irving must know about German governmental genocide. **—Delloyd J. Guth, Ph.D.**
*Professor of Law and Director of the Canadian Legal History Project
University of Manitoba*